What Others Are .
Child Care Busin

"If you are truly motivated to build a successful child care center, don't put down this inspirational book until you reach the last page. Whether dealing with keeping your center full, inspiring or retaining your staff, the stories in here will give you invaluable insights and contribute to your success. I wish I had this book 25 years ago as we were getting started."

Ty Durekas, Co-Founder, Children's Creative Learning Center

"Julie Bartkus is an inspiration; it is no wonder so many people wanted to be a part of this book! *Child Care Business Success* is a telling work, genuinely motivated by Julie's vision to support child care owners as they strive to uplevel their businesses. With every story shared in this book, you'll be inspired to make your vision your reality. Julie has a personal, heartfelt approach to getting to the root of the real needs in child care while supporting her clients with her easy-to-follow Child Care Business Success Model. With every page you read it will become clearer and clearer that what you desire is possible!"

Dena AuCoin, Kaplan University

"Julie Bartkus has written a masterpiece that should be put into the hands of every child care business owner and director. Her insightful interviews and easy-to-follow success model make this book a gem. Her book is awesome and one I simply couldn't stop reading!"

Regina Miller, Owner, Princeton Children's Center

"Being mentored by Julie Bartkus has brought me so many gains, both professionally as a child care business owner and personally. As I've implemented her strategies over these past two years that we've been working together, I've seen a transformation in my business that I didn't even know was possible. In the first three weeks alone we enrolled thirty-six children—far more than we ever had enrolled before in that short of a time.

"But the benefits far exceed enrollment. My vision has become a powerful force in our program. Families recognize a difference in our program and want to be part of what we offer. Our teaching team has become more professional and aligned with the vision of the company to wrap our arms around our families. We no longer struggle with petty problems, but instead forge pathways to new levels of excellence. In one year we went from a program with a provisional license to a four-star program, and we have increased revenues for our single site by over $200,000 per year.

"As I read this book I recognized so much of what Julie taught me through her mentoring. I know this book will have a powerful impact on other child care business owners and directors who are looking for a way to reach much higher goals in their child care businesses."

Mary Wardlaw, Owner, The Children's Center

"Julie Bartkus understands the big issues that truly make the difference for child care business success–having a vision and culture that motivate an empowered team of people. This book helps bring these critical concepts to life with powerful, real-world case studies."

Ron Spreeuwenberg, Co-Founder and CEO, HiMama

"This is by far the BEST book about child care business success that I have read! If your goal is to write your own success story in the child care industry, this book will give you all the tools you need. Julie Bartkus is passionate, inspiring and dedicated to helping others transform their mindset in order to achieve success. The strength of positive and productive relationships is central to the content found within these pages. Julie begins by clearly defining her Child Care Business Success model and keeps the conversation moving along as experts in the industry share what matters most to the decisions they make on a daily basis. The information presented will motivate you to rethink how you operate your business, prioritize your actions, build lasting relationships, retain a dedicated staff and impact the families you serve."

Dianne Baker–Educator, Consultant, Trainer, Curriculum Developer

"Julie has a real gift for helping others find and refine their vision. Then, she jumps in to help make that vision a reality. Identifying and implementing the right strategies in your business happens much more quickly and with greater success when you work with a great coach like her. And, even more important, she is able to help business owners dig deep within themselves to get clear on their personal goals and desired outcomes. This book will help you start the journey, and Julie is ready to help you along the way."

Jeff Fisher, President, Local Child Care Marketing

"I've seen child care facilities turn around with Julie's help and without it, and I can tell you, unequivocally, the process is a lot faster and less painful with Julie!

"Of course, Julie's Child Care Business Success program provides you with the tools and the knowledge you'll need to grow your business. But, you know what?—a lot of programs do that. What sets Julie apart is the passion and inspiration she brings to the project. Working in a small business, I appreciate this. I understand that it's not possible to implement every suggested improvement, but without passion and enthusiasm, whatever you do is going to fall flat. The flip side, of course, is that no matter how enthusiastic you are about your business, you also must have the tools to make it successful. Julie is going to teach you both.

"I've met very successful preschool owners who come back to Julie every single year, which has always impressed me. A business model based on teaching other people how to be successful usually is sustainable only through acquiring new clients (the hardest kind to get!), because the old clients don't need you anymore. When I asked Julie's extremely successful clients why they keep coming back, every single one told me some version of this: 'We need the occasional reminder that we do this because we love it. Julie gives us that reminder along with the ever-changing tools we need to compete in this crazy competitive market.' If that's not a ringing endorsement of Julie's ability to change your business, I don't know what is."

Stacey Coleman, Vice President of Operations, Preschool2me

"Simple things matter. Simple things like listening to and honoring our heart's desire matter. Simple things like learning from the heartbreak of loss matter. Simple things like telling our own truth and believing ourselves, these matter. Why? Because our truth sets us free.

"How easily busy-ness can elbow out what matters. Our business as child care leaders is to change the world. To make our world better for children and families. Busy-ness can never begin to fuel the passion we need to create and run a business intent upon making the world better for children. If you have been drowning in busy-ness, you need to pick up Julie Bartkus' book, the one that every child care business owner is waiting for. The truth-telling in Julie's book will set you free from busy-ness and put you on the track toward fulfillment.

"Julie poignantly reminds us that no one else can live our life for us. So why do we pay attention to the perfectionist committee in our heads that berates us for what we should have done? How can we fire the 'should-ers' and hire the 'can-doers'? If you want a coach who will stand by you as you reclaim your own path, your own vision and your promise since birth, that coach is waiting for you.

"In fact, Julie Bartkus offers you a team of everyday miracle workers who, like you, simply want to make the world better for children by creating your own thriving business. Are you ready to be inspired? Are you ready to find the support you've always yearned for? If these hard-working folk can do it, you can too. Read Julie's book. What have you got to lose?"

Holly Elissa Bruno, M.A., J.D., Award-Winning and Best-Selling Author, International Keynoter, Radio Host

Child Care Business Success

Julie Bartkus

Child Care Business Success

Create your positive, productive and profitable child care business!

Featuring Educational Playcare, Wee School, Children's Lighthouse, Brandi's Place, Munchkin Manor, Appletree Day Care, Hildebrandt Learning Centers and more.

Positive Press

Spring Grove, IL

Published by Positive Press
Spring Grove, IL

Cover and Interior Design by Imagine! Studios
www.ArtsImagine.com

Cover Photo: Pro777/Dreamstime.com

ISBN: 978-0-9777215-0-4 (paperback)
ISBN: 978-0-9777215-1-1 (e-book)

Library of Congress Control Number: 2017941849

First Positive Press printing: June 2017

Dedication &
Acknowledgements

This book is dedicated to child care business owners around the world who built their child care businesses out of their desire to give the children of our world a high-quality early learning experience, not to mention an abundance of love and hugs. It's been my pleasure hearing your stories and being a part of your journeys.

I'd also like to give a big shout-out to our sponsors who have joined forces with me to make this book and The Child Care Business Success Movement a reality. Our sponsors are businesses that support your child care business success and include: Childcare CRM, EZCare, Power Web Videos, Preschool2Me, Watch Me Grow and ChildCareIRiS.

Special appreciation goes out to two people who helped me bring this book from conceptualization to completion. Martha Rasche, I appreciate every single read-through you did to help this book be grammatically correct and polished. You helped me tremendously with your never-ending enthusiasm for the book's content and my vision. I truly appreciate you. Joe Eckstein, your guidance with every step of the process in making this book into a beautiful, thoughtful publication for the child care industry was invaluable. You cheered me on and helped me simplify the process while bringing *Child Care Business Success* to life. Our partnership to create the beautiful cover and layout was a successful one. Thank you so very much.

In order to achieve success, you've got to have mentors and business strategists. Being a business owner is tough when you're walking alone. I encourage all of you reading this to find a coach or a mentor who resonates with you and who consistently challenges your mindset. I'd like to thank a few of mine, including David Neagle, Jim Palmer, Steve Sipress, Phil Dyer and Angelique Rewers. Each one of you has played such a critical role in my growth and in showing me what's possible. I'm incredibly grateful and can't wait for what the future will bring forth.

To people in my mastermind groups who are there with support and solid advice: If my entire journey here on this planet was so that I could get to know you, the journey has been well worth it. Special hugs and love to my "Round Table." You all shine so brightly!

To my biggest fan, my mom, Vicki Bartkus: As I get older, I grow with wisdom as to the tremendous gift that you have given to me, which is my life, first and foremost, but also just by you being who you need to be in this life so that I can be who I need to be. At times you are my biggest teacher, while at other times you are simply my biggest fan. I love you.

And last but certainly not least, my Tom. Thank you for being so excited every time we danced. Thank you for showing your support and enthusiasm for every word I wrote. It was your back that sprouted wings way before mine ever did, and I'm so enlightened that I got to experience your journey. I love you in a way that extends far beyond our worldly existence, and I am so very grateful for the dance we shared in this little thing called life.

Access The Child Care Business Success Book Vault!

Hear the full interviews from this book on audio and more!

Scan this code:

Visit:

www.ChildCareBusinessSuccessBookVault.com

Password: RockMyChildCare.com

Contents

Meet Julie's friends in the back of this book.

They support your child care business success and have some special gifts for you!

*Please note: Since the time of Julie's interviews with each of the featured guests, things may have changed. Some owners expanded their centers while others pursued greater passions. When possible, an update has been included at the conclusion of each chapter. Interviews were facilitated from 2012 to 2013.

Introduction

My Discovery of This One Thing
That Changes Everything

It was in May of 2012 that everything changed for me. I was standing in the middle of my old, beat-up house that had been built in 1904. My husband, Tom, and I had bought it to remodel so his parents could enjoy a worry-free, freshly remodeled space in which to live out their lives. Unfortunately, this day was different from all of the others that we had shared in our marriage. It was our last day together, just a week short of our four-year wedding anniversary. I stood there all alone, in the middle of my living room, surrounded by Tom's paintings and the couch where I had often fallen asleep as Tom rubbed my feet. I didn't want this day to end. I thought over and over in my mind: *How did I get here?*

One year earlier, while we were remodeling our house, Tom's dad passed away, and we moved his mom right in to live with us even though the downstairs apartment wasn't completely finished. Tom was very persistent that she needed to be with us now. At the time I didn't get his sense of urgency, not only for this but also for many things he did, but I agreed. We formed our new, close-knit family: a bunny; my dog, Teddy; my mother-in-law, Dori; my stepson, Mason; and Tom and me, all under one roof. Plus my mother-in-law came with three cats.

I want to tell you something about Mason. When Tom and I first became serious in our relationship, I decided I would hold a special place for Mason in my heart and love him like he was my own son. I thought it was cute that his name was only one letter away from spelling *my son*. He was my son. Not that he didn't have another mom, his real mom. He did. It was just a decision I made. I made another decision too, and that was to love his real mom through his eyes—not mine and not Tom's—but through Mason's eyes.

My home was full with love and lots of food. I often thought it was funny that when I decided to make a big dinner, Dori would walk in with a bucket of hot chicken ready to be devoured. In the evenings Tom perfected his recipes for popovers and apple pie. In the moments when I smelled the aromas of amazing food overflowing from the kitchen into the entire house, my heart was full, knowing my home was filled with lots of love.

Tom knew from the moment he reconnected with me online in 2006 that he wanted to marry me. I had no clue. I was living in Massachusetts at the time and was just ending a long relationship with a wonderful person. We just weren't growing together, so I decided to move back home to Northern Illinois, to be closer to my family after being away for a good ten years.

I had known Tom in high school, and as kids growing up, we lived in the same neighborhood. I can't remember the exact moment that we met, but I do remember him being at my birthday parties from the time I was fifteen. We danced together in school, and years later, after we reconnected, I found my diary and read my early entries where I wrote about our friendship and how Tom wanted to go out with me and, well, I just thought he was a little pushy. We went out only once, to our homecoming bonfire, but we continued to hang out and dance together in high school dance shows and musicals. After we parted ways, I always reflected back on those times, knowing that they were some of the most special times I would have in my life.

One fateful day, all of my special memories came fluttering back into my heart, after Tom reached out to me through

Classmates.com. I didn't recognize his first name because I had known him as Tom, and through Classmates.com someone named Ranchford was trying to contact me. He also e-mailed my older sister, Deb, whom he was friends with, and she sent me an e-mail asking, "Is this our Tom?" I asked him about his name, and he said he had used his middle name in high school because he felt like his given name, Ranchford, was only one step better than being named Rumpelstiltskin.

Tom took me out on a date and brought me back to his house. I asked him for a drink of water. He turned the faucet on and was attempting to fill my glass when he looked back at me, got down on one knee and proposed. I was in total shock and said, "Are you crazy?" He said, "I just know we're supposed to be married." I said, "I just ended a ten-year relationship." Thankfully, he got up and let the subject rest. Every day for about a year, he proposed. Sometimes twice. I kept saying, "Not today," "Not today." Then finally one day, he asked and I said yes. He was over-the-top excited, like a little boy who had just heard from his parents that they were going to Disneyland.

So on June 7, 2008, we got married with our son, Mason, standing up for him and my niece Amber standing up for me. I married my dance partner, a boy I had known since I was fifteen. Tom and I loved our wedding date: 6,7,8. We knew we'd never, ever forget it.

Back to May 2012. It was one week short of our four-year wedding anniversary, and it was time for me to hop on a teleconference call and teach a group of child care directors how to eliminate gossip in their workplaces. Tom made me dinner. It was an amazingly yummy breakfast burrito, which I loved. I ate fast, put my plate down on the counter and headed into my office to make my call. "See you in an hour or so," Tom said. Then he headed out to the garage to work on one of his masterpieces.

I had been on my call for just under sixty minutes when all of a sudden someone started pounding on my office door. I tried to ignore it and continued teaching. I didn't even think that perhaps something urgent was going on. In fact, I felt a little annoyed that I was being interrupted. I wrapped up my call, unlocked my door and headed through the dining room into the kitchen. I heard my neighbor downstairs telling my mother-in-law, "Sit down. It's going to be okay." I thought, *Oh, no. She fell and broke her hip.* Tom and I often talked about how to make it safer for Dori to get to the downstairs apartment.

My neighbor Dan came upstairs and said, "Julie, it's Tom." I said, "What?" "It's Tom, and it's not good." I thought, *Crap. He fell out of a tree*, because he was working on cutting the limbs down. My mind was racing with so many thoughts. "No," Dan said, "Tom's on the porch." I walked out to the porch and saw Michelle, Dan's wife, giving CPR to Tom, who was stretched out on the deck. Teddy, our dog, was outside with him, and his coffee was still warm on the porch step where he had been sitting just before several neighbors came over because something just didn't look right. Michelle looked up at me and said, "He's not breathing."

I was in shock, looking at my husband and his lifeless body. *He's not breathing. I didn't even kiss him or say thank you for my dinner. He's not breathing. Can life really change in a minute? Was this the end? How did I get here?* I started crying, telling Tom to come back, looking at my neighbor Holly, telling her he can come back if he wants to. I thought about Mason and about how he had moved out several weeks earlier and not spoken to his father since.

The ambulance came to take Tom to the hospital. I made the ambulance workers promise not to stop trying to help him. Holly and I followed the ambulance, and after we waited at the hospital, the doctor came out. "I'm sorry. There's nothing I could do. We tried." "What? You're telling me he's gone?" "Yes. I'm sorry." Tom, my dance partner, was gone.

I went back to my old 1904 house and stood there in the middle of my living room, looking at everything Tom had left behind, thinking, *How did I get here? What now?*

The day Tom died from a fatal heart attack at age forty-seven was the longest day of my life. Literally. I didn't want to sleep, so I stayed awake, waiting for a neighbor or family member to wake up. I called people and talked to their answering machines at two o'clock in the morning. I simply didn't want the last day that Tom had been alive to end.

For several months after Tom passed away, I worked hard to reclaim my life. I needed to figure out how to move on as a single gal. I always had been in long-term relationships. Always had that sense of security around me. Always had people to take care of. And now it felt like my entire WHY, my entire reason for existing, had been stripped away from me.

Mason no longer lived with me and within a couple weeks after Tom's passing, Dori panicked and decided to move out and live with her daughter. A life I had built for everyone else around me was now solely mine. Did I even want it?

I had so many questions. *How do I move forward? How do I live alone?* I could write an entire book solely about my journey from May 2012 to now, but the key wisdom I gained was that there's one thing that will carry you through. There's one thing that will transform your life personally and professionally.

And this one thing—is the secret sauce to having a DREAMY, passion-driven life. It's also the one thing that makes everything else work, and it's the one thing that is missing from many people's lives. It has the power to transform child care programs, including filling enrollments in record time, attracting and retaining

DREAMY staff and clients, and sustaining a motivated and dynamic team. It allows child care owners to experience the time, freedom and profits that they desire, and, most importantly, deserve. It's the one thing that kept me living, and the one reason I'm here today writing this book.

Are you ready to discover the power of this one thing and get really DREAMY with your child care business . . . and your life?

So what is this one thing? I'll end the suspense and tell you. **It's your vision.** Your vision for your life and your vision for your child care business. If you're like me and most business owners out there, you have a vision. But the big question is, Are you living in your vision? This is a question that one of my mentors, David Neagle, always asked me. He would say, "Julie, yes, you have a vision—but are you living in it?" Whenever he said that to me, I got a little perturbed trying to understand the difference. He wouldn't directly tell me, he would just ask me questions so that I could reveal the answers to myself. He knew that if I revealed the answers on my own, I would discover the profound truth that would change my life.

My story of my life with Tom reflects back to me many of the stories that I've heard in my almost twenty years of working side by side with child care business owners. Most owners are women who want to provide a quality child care experience for their children and the children in the community. There is a vision at the onset of their—your—child care business, and then the daily stress takes over and becomes the guiding force for how the day unfolds. The vision starts to deflate. You then find yourself doing everything for everyone else, tolerating situations and circumstances, hoping and believing that people will be there for you. Then you find out that in a quick moment staff can depart and clients can go somewhere else, and all the energy that you put out there only leaves you having to give more to keep your child care business running. Your big, bold, dreamy vision fades away and is replaced by just trying to survive the daily stress, and everything seems hard. Personally and professionally, it's a struggle.

This book is designed to help you reconnect with your vision and feel on fire about your life, personally and professionally. Then, from that place deep within yourself, you'll be able to up-level your success and start living in your vision, as opposed to just having a vision in place. All that's required to begin this transformational journey is a shift in perception. This book, as well as all of my work with child care owners, directors and teams, will propel you to a new thought process that will leave you thinking: *It's Possible!* There's a lot of strategies in this book. But as with any deep transformation you desire, it's so much more than just collecting strategies. Many of my child care clients from around the world tell me about their Julie Bartkus file cabinet where they store all of the ideas that I've shared with them throughout the years.

My belief in achieving greater levels of child care business success is that you have to do more than collect great strategies. You need to implement action; the right action. But often we get stuck and don't implement the strategies that will lead to greater success and then we look for a different idea to implement. I've seen over and over again that strategy plus strategy typically leaves a business owner needing more and more strategy. But if you do a deep dive, and allow yourself the experience of a personal transformation to overcome the places where you're stuck, and then add effective strategy to that, you'll get long-lasting, positive results. And that's what I want for each one of you— long-lasting, positive results.

My journey with Tom awakened me to a deeper place that I needed to function from to change my life. For me, Tom's passing was like hitting rock bottom at lightning speed. I built my life around doing everything that everyone else wanted, only to be left alone in an old farmhouse that we purchased for someone else. Everyone else's desires were the things I wanted to make happen. When everyone was gone, I was left thinking, *What do I desire? What do I really want? How do I tap into those things after doing everything for everyone else for so long?* Everyone else was my vision, or so I thought. In reality my vision needed to be reawakened so I could let everything else flow from me authentically and genuinely, so I could really find me and the vision that I would truly, deeply, passionately live in.

Do you feel like your journey has brought you to the same place? Are you left wondering, *How do I transition out of managing my day by the daily stress?* Whether that means low enrollments, not enough money or a lack of motivated staff, those issues, for most child care business owners, become the daily stress. Plus in the child care industry it's so easy to live your life for everyone else. For the parents, the children, your staff, your spouse. Your vision becomes seeing them happy. Maybe you're left asking yourself the question, *How did I get here?*

When I started reawakening my vision, it started expanding. My starting point was to pay attention to my desires, to the things that made me uniquely me. So I created a "desire wall" where I took five-by-seven sticky notes, and every time I felt a desire inside of myself, I wrote it down and posted it on a special wall in my office. I did not judge my desires as good or bad or too expensive. I just acknowledged them and added them to the wall. Soon I had an entire wall covered in sticky notes containing the desires that I felt in my heart. Soon I was getting reconnected with *me*. My desires included simple things like skirts and boots and midnight swims, to more elaborate things like diamond earrings. The key was to pay attention and write down my desires.

Several months later, I took a nap in the afternoon, and I awoke with this vision that set me on fire. So much so that I took out a piece of paper and scribbled down all of the ideas that came to me so I wouldn't forget them. I was excited and started sharing my vision with several people, and they got excited and invested in it right away. I was in awe as to how quickly people could be moved to buy into your vision if you're truly—authentically and genuinely—excited about it and you feel a sense of urgency that this has to happen! All I did was pick up the phone and have conversations with people about my vision. That's it.

The same thing is true for your child care program. If you're on fire with a BIG, BOLD vision and you have a sense of urgency to make it happen, those enrollments will get filled. Those open positions will get filled. Your profits will soar!

The vision that was awakened within me was to create a movement—a Child Care Business Success Movement where I, along with several sponsors, could wrap my arms around child care owners and give them support. The vision that I had came to me with very specific details: Create a book sharing stories of child care business success and others who brought their big visions to life. Then create a website where all of the interviews I would feature in the book could be heard and the transcripts could be downloaded. Then go out and be with owners and take your book on the road with you.

And I tell you what, when a vision is laid out for you and you clearly see the steps in your mind's eye, you see it as if it's already happened. Then as you progress toward the end result, you'll be tested. People will challenge you. The plan will take longer to implement. You'll hit roadblocks. Almost as if someone is asking you, "Do you really want this? How bad do you want this? Will you take decisive action to make what you want to have happen, happen?" If you move through the roadblocks, navigate through the struggle, you'll come out on the other side living deeper in your vision every single day. And when you do it right, your vision will always be in a state of expansion, never stagnating.

I'm delighted to share with you this book which is a big part of my vision. In addition to this publication, we have a website waiting for you to visit where you can download the full transcripts and listen to the audio interviews that make up this book. You'll also find my tour schedule so that you can join me live and uplevel your child care business and your life with strategies that my clients implement, to experience transformational results in record time.

But rest assured, you'll receive tons of strategies and hear some amazing stories that will help you get to the next level of where you want to grow, right in this book.

These stories are critically important for me to share with you. Many of our owners whose stories are shared here have never told them before. Pay close attention to how you feel when you read the stories, because it's our stories that engage people on a deep level with our visions. And a mistake that many child care owners make is not sharing their stories that allow parents and staff and the community to really connect with them. And when it comes to buying decisions—meaning, where a parent is going to enroll his or her child or where a potential dreamy staff member is going to work—it is an emotional decision. It's a decision that is made based on emotional connections.

Before we dive into the first chapter of this book where I share with you my Child Care Business Success Model, I want to thank the sponsors who made this book possible and give a special shout-out to three owners: Vernon Mason, Jr., Sindye Alexander and Carolyn Driggers. Thank you. Thank you for seeing the vision, and thank you for patiently waiting while we rolled the book out and into the hands of child care owners and directors across the globe. Your stories are absolutely inspiring, and I know you'll leave a legacy with the businesses you created and also because you decided to share your stories in this one-of-a-kind book to benefit the child care industry.

Chapter 1

Julie's Child Care Business Success Model

"Don't underestimate the power of a vision. McDonald's founder Ray Kroc pictured his empire long before it existed, and he saw how to get there. He invented the company motto—'Quality, service, cleanliness and value'—and kept repeating it to employees for the rest of his life."

Kenneth Labich

When you think about upleveling your child care business success, it's important to get clear on what it is that you really want to have happen, and then pinpoint the action that will get you there. As simple as these two steps sound, they are the areas that many child care owners struggle with.

In the next chapters, you'll discover stories of child care owners who brought their big visions to life as they reveal the strategies that they implemented to achieve tremendous results.

When you finish reading this book, you might ask yourself, *Where do I start?*, because there's a lot of transformational information packed into this book. So I figured Chapter 1 is the perfect place to share with you my model for child care business success that has been helping child care owners uplevel their success for almost twenty years.

I developed this model after many child care owners approached me wanting to change the results they were getting in their child care programs. They wanted a motivated staff. They wanted to find out the most effective ways for attracting and retaining the best child care staff and clients. They wanted full enrollments. They wanted more profits. And whenever our initial consultations began, it seemed the owners isolated each result they wanted to experience as a separate piece and were looking for the quick fixes for each symptom they were experiencing.

For example, if enrollments were not filled, they wanted marketing ideas. If staff were negative, they wanted team-building activities that would alter their moods. If profits were not high enough, they wanted a strategy to keep more of what they made.

What I quickly discovered was missing was a holistic approach to achieving greater levels of child care business success, an approach that looks at the picture as a whole and acknowledges that everything is interrelated and codependent on each other. This is a different approach than just treating the symptoms, or what I call putting a Band-Aid over the problem, so that you get the quickest relief possible. It's really tough to stay in business and be profitable and authentically and genuinely happy in that business if all you do is treat the symptoms. And I tell you what, Band-Aid solutions, although they might seem the cheapest solutions, will cost you more in the long run. A lot more.

Let's take the component of staff motivation. You say, "My staff are unmotivated. Let's get someone in here to motivate them." Then you invest money in a team-building day, and you see results for a few days, and then everyone goes back to how they were before the team-building program. That money was pretty much wasted because you didn't see any long-lasting, positive results. Plus, when staff are not motivated, additional profits are dripping out of your pocket because your staff are not your raving fans. They are not spreading the positive word of mouth far, fast and furious about your child care program. They might actually be doing the opposite, which in the long run will cost you lots of money. This is all regardless of the fantastic referral program you have in place, which also took you time and money to develop, and it's not availing you much results.

Just for fun, let's list all the additional ways unmotivated staff are killing your profits. Go ahead and check the items below that you can relate to!

The not-so-common things to think about include the following:

- ☐ Your own **negative thoughts about staff**. (One negative thought can lead to eight hours of procrastination!)
- ☐ You **tolerating behavioral issues.**
- ☐ You **hanging on to the wrong staff** for too long.
- ☐ You **not upleveling the staff you have in place** to serve your clients.
- ☐ You **managing your program by your fears** of not finding good staff. (This is BIG!)
- ☐ You **buying into what others in the industry say about finding good staff**.
- ☐ Your mental energy **being drained by staff issues** so you are not focused on ways to keep your big vision alive and growing.

- ☐ You **not sleeping well** because you're up all hours of the night thinking about staff and the challenges you're facing.

- ☐ You **not being a RAVING fan of your child care program** on social media.

- ☐ **Staff not being raving fans** of yours in any capacity. (Along with you, they should be your best marketers.)

- ☐ You feeling like you have to **pull the curtains closed when parents or potential new staff come in** to meet you so the true happenings among staff are not exposed.

- ☐ You hiding and **not building positive and proactive relationships with the community** that you serve so you stand out as THE child care program of choice.

- ☐ You feeling less than, maybe even **fearing, your competition** because you know the true inner workings of your child care program.

- ☐ You **not knowing how to find good staff**. Scratch that. You not knowing how to find DREAMY staff.

- ☐ You **feeling overwhelmed**.

- ☐ You **wearing too many hats**.

- ☐ **Staff judging** new families and other staff members.

- ☐ **Staff not building positive and proactive relationships** with the child care community you are trying so hard to build.

- ☐ You **not delegating**.

- ☐ You **not letting go of control**.

- ☐ You knowing there's an internal shift you need to make but **you feel stuck** when trying to figure it out or overcome it on your own.

These are just some of the hard-hitting truths about how "staff" issues kill your profits. How many items on this list can you relate to?

These things are tricky to think about, because your profit that's being killed is slowly dripping out of your pocket and does not appear directly on your profit and loss statements. So there's no line item that says *Unmotivated Staff*. But you feel it and see it in the results your program is getting. Even if you have enough strategy in place to keep your pipeline filled with clients, you might be experiencing high turnover in parents, not realizing their lifetime value.

I encourage you to think about the impact that each one of the listed items has on everything else. Think about how the staff you have in place impact your marketing. And how they impact your profits. And how they impact your ability to attract new team members to work for you.

So when I work with child care owners like you, we look at the whole picture and use my Child Care Business Success Model to pinpoint where we need to start to get you the results that you desire and that you deserve. This empowers us to understand the cause of the effect that you're experiencing so you can move beyond just treating the symptom and treat the root cause. Once you take action that's in alignment with my model, you'll get to experience long-lasting, positive change!

One of my amazing clients is Mary Wardlaw. She has achieved phenomenal results during our work together so far, like getting thirty-six enrollments in three weeks! Or eliminating more than two million dollars in profit killers. You can listen to her story at **www.ChildCareBusinessSuccess.com**.

Let's dive into my model and see how you can use it to achieve greater levels of child care business success.

Julie Bartkus'
Child Care Business Success Model

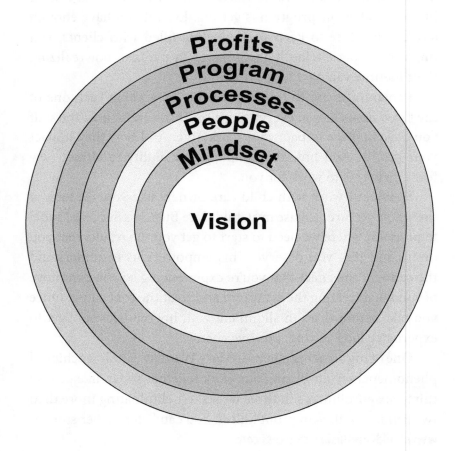

The one factor that changes everything that I wrote about in my introduction is at the center of my model. It's your **vision**. I spend a great deal of time working with my clients on this piece because it's crucial to making everything else in your child care business work. I want you to think about each of the rings in my model being interdependent on the ring before it. So if we remove the center ring—your **vision**—what happens to all of the other rings?

If you guessed that they'll collapse, you are correct. My model works its way from the center out. We have to get your vision in place, good and strong to support everything else. Then we have to develop the correct **mindset** that supports your vision. Your people create the environment that you're engulfed in daily, and if your **people** are not so dreamy, your mindset will expand only so far. Those are three crucial pieces of my holistic approach to achieving greater levels of child care business success. And even though they are the most crucial, they are the most neglected. If you're like many child care owners, you had a vision at the onset of creating your child care business, but then life happened, and your vision got filed away or taped to a wall or simply forgotten about after the words had been written. At some point the business stops expanding, starts dying, and the daily stress (and your fears) takes over as the guiding force for your organization. And then you step back and wonder, *Why is everyone lacking motivation?* The realization has to be made that your staff will never be more inspired about your child care program than the inspiration you feel yourself. So when leaders in the industry ask me, "Julie, how do we get staff to feel motivated and energized coming into work in the morning?," I in turn ask them, "How motivated and energized do you feel coming into work in the morning?"

I'm not talking about a "smile on a stick" kind of motivated and inspired. I'm talking about real, authentic, genuine and positive energy that radiates out of your being because you are living in your vision, and it is BIG, BOLD and super DREAMY. A smile on a stick, on the other hand, is when you know you have to be motivated, so you pump yourself up, put on that proverbial fake smile and keep it there until the parent leaves or the interview is over. This is a tough way to create a successful child care business. It's a lot of work, and you'll feel the struggle. You'll feel the hardship as you try endlessly to make it all work. Maybe you feel the struggle now.

The next component in my model is your **processes**. Processes support your people, who support your mindset, which supports your vision. Processes range from staff motivation techniques, such as your staff meetings, team meetings and one-on-one meetings, to your hiring procedures. They run wide from your business-relationship-building strategies to your marketing plan of action. Processes make life easier, and they need to support the first three components of the model: your vision, your mindset and your people.

I had one client who loved her processes. And she was incredibly strong at developing them and enforcing them. But the other three rings of her model were very weak, so she found herself having to police her staff to follow the policies and procedures as opposed to letting the policies and procedures support her people. There's a big difference, and you'll feel it in the results that you experience.

The next rings in the model represent your **program** and then your **profits**. Once you work the model in the correct order from the inside out, your end result is a fantastic program with high profits. Then the super cool thing happens—you have more profits to fuel everything else! It's an amazing dynamic to see change as owners work through my model. The way many owners do it is to focus on the outer two rings and neglect the inner three rings, so they never get to experience the results that their child care program is really capable of.

When enrollments are low, owners start comparing what they have to offer with what their perceived competition has to offer, and they come to the conclusion that they need to buy something as opposed to reinvigorating the vision and expanding it daily. To me it's really interesting how our minds default to the wrong action we need to take to revitalize our child care businesses. This is why a coach or a mentor is crucial to your child care business success, and I encourage you to find a coach who you resonate with and one who challenges your mindset. There was a quote that I once heard and will never forget that says essentially, "If you're in the picture, you can't see the picture." You need someone who is capable of seeing the big picture and all of the working pieces, so you can grow.

Your mindset, the second ring in my model, is crucial for expanding and upleveling so that each day you experience the results you desire. It's important to note that you will never accomplish more than your mindset dictates is possible. If you rule out possibilities, guess what? You'll prove yourself absolutely correct. When I started deep-diving into my own mindset well over twenty years ago, I made a few monumental discoveries. First, you have a default mindset setting where your thoughts stem from. Whenever you're faced with a challenge or a crisis, your mindset will go right to the thoughts that were fed to you from the time you took in your first breath of life. Prior to the age of seven, your mind was a sponge that absorbed what everyone else said about money, about relationships, about yourself, about sex, about spirituality. They may have given you messages directly, or you observed how they felt about certain matters and then you took on those feelings as your own.

The challenge becomes to break out of the thoughts that were programmed into you and start thinking new thoughts, thoughts that might even feel crazy to think. But they are thoughts that support your vision. And to some degree, over time, you've had new thoughts about certain situations but definitely not all situations. This leaves room to continuously expand your mindset daily. The problem that comes up is that if you're not expanding your mindset daily in support of your vision, your mindset contracts back to its original state of being. Think of your mind like a computer.

A computer has an operating system. That operating system doesn't change regardless of what program we try to run on it. It simply defaults back to its standard mode of operation. That's what our minds do. And the more you expand your mindset and believe in the possibilities of your BIG vision, the bigger the results you're going to begin experiencing.

The biggest challenge for most child care owners when it comes to mindset is having the right people in place who support success. Most mindsets support neediness and fear, as opposed to success and empowerment. This is a main reason I created our mentorship community, so that your mindset can be challenged to expand in the direction of the results you desire to experience. I recently wrote an article at LinkedIn, titled "How Giraffes Boost Your Profits." Here's an excerpt.

How Giraffes Boost Your Profits

This is an unconventional approach to boosting profits in your child care program. But it's absolutely true—hanging out with Giraffes boosts your profits. As a matter of fact, when you're not surrounded by Giraffes, you're actually killing your profit potential.

Now, before you go running off to the zoo, let me explain.

A Giraffe is what my coaching clients and Child Care Program of Excellence Mentorship members call the high-level visionary space that child care owners need to occupy in order to achieve maximum growth in their child care programs. I'll confess, I started it with my child care clients, but it originated from Bishop T. D. Jakes.

We introduced the concept of Giraffes and Turtles at the first annual Child Care Business Success Conference, and it stuck with our clients and mentorship members ever since.

So I thought I would share the concept with you. You see, in order to experience exponential growth in your child care program, you need to be the high-level visionary. Your reach of what you can "see" needs to far outreach what anyone else can possibly "see."

But there's a problem.

You're surrounded by Turtles. Turtles are great, don't get me wrong, but their reach is limited by their shells. They can stretch their necks out only so far and see only so high. Turtles are your staff, other child care professionals in your community with limited mindset and even your family. Turtles are people who make you feel like things aren't possible and your dream is a little crazy.

Turtles might be people who state:

"This is only child care." Or,

"There's no decent staff out there." Or,

"There are not enough families to enroll."

And the list goes on.

The problem is that Turtles don't ever reach the height of the Giraffe. They don't climb up trees so they can "see" what a Giraffe "sees."

However, the Giraffe will bend her neck down to ground level, compromising her stance, to take on the Turtle's perspective. When this happens the Giraffe's BIG vision begins to crumble, and she begins to think and act like a Turtle, forgetting she is a Giraffe.

To boost your profits and experience exponential growth, you need a community of Giraffes to continuously hold you to a higher standard, to remind you that you are a Giraffe.

That's why hanging out with Giraffes will boost your profits. It will help you stay in the right visionary state of mind so you can take the BIG steps you need to take to grow your child care program.

I always say that the toughest thing about bringing the change you want to see is your mindset. It's the thoughts you think that determine the actions you take, and that determines your results. So often child care owners and directors have fantastic strategies, but their mindset to support the strategies is the missing piece. The same is true for your staff. Maybe you've had the experience where you give them training on conflict resolution, and the strategy is brilliant and it's worked for so many others, yet for some reason your staff don't implement what they learned. The toughest obstacle to staff motivation and the toughest obstacle to building a successful child care business is what goes on between your two ears. It's your thoughts and your mindset.

During my live mentorship meetings, I have my owners and directors create what I call "power thoughts." These are dreamy thoughts of what they truly want to experience in their child care programs. I have them write down their thoughts and read them out loud, putting boatloads of enthusiasm into their words. We hone in on around thirty thoughts that we work on expanding in our minds, so that our actions follow suit and we experience the thoughts come into reality. It's quite powerful.

At one of our last meetings, my client Mary shared with the group that all of the thoughts that she had written down had not been true at that time, but now, several months after consistently focusing on them, consistently expanding them, they are true! Our power thoughts have to do with the results we want to experience. They are thoughts you can decide to think in spite of the fact that you're not yet experiencing the results. Some of my group's power thoughts include:

I always attract amazing people to work for me.

I am fully enrolled with a waiting list.

I fall deeper in love with what I do every day.

I am worth it.

It's the power of your mindset that will carry you through and help you achieve results in record time. I'm consistently challenging my clients to think beyond their perceived limitations. If they say, "Julie, I can enroll twelve kids in the next four months," I say, "Why not twenty-four in the next month?" Their response, "Nobody ever told me it was possible." The truth is that right now, in this moment, you're creating your own world of possibilities by what your mindset dictates is possible and the actions that you take to support your own world of possibilities. If a client says, "Julie, nobody in the industry enrolls that many kids during this time of the year," I ask, "Do you want to think like everyone else, or do you want to raise the bar for what you make possible in your own life?"

If you study the mindset of a millionaire, you'll find that it is much different than a middle-class mindset. As a matter of fact, when businesses were collapsing during the Great Depression, some people were creating million-dollar business. So you can take charge of your own mindset and your own world of possibilities, or you can buy into the status quo and experience the same results you've always gotten, or the results that other people tell you is possible. The choice is yours.

The one element that changes everything is your vision, the center of my model. When I mentor clients privately or through my Child Care Program of Excellence Mentorship, I give them specific steps to bring their visions back to life so it returns to being the guiding force for business growth. It's the one thing that needs to be expanding daily so your business thrives. You can have a strong, compelling vision and sell people on the idea of what you want to create, of what type of child care program you want to bring into existence, and you can fill your business and have a waiting list before there's even a physical building. But first you must have a BIG vision and, second, have the mindset that dictates that it is indeed possible.

I love studying visionaries and what they've made happen during their lifetimes, and what continued to transpire after their passing, because they were on fire with big visions. People like Maria Montessori. Maria passed away in 1952, and to this date she is still inspiring people to buy into the Montessori ways. Several of my Montessori clients shared with me that they watched a video of her speaking and were inspired to start a Montessori school. Approximately sixty-five years after her death, and her vision is still inspiring so many people.

Then there's Susan B. Anthony, who had a vision that women would have the right to vote. She was driven with urgency that it had to happen, that our country needed to see this change take place. She put suffrage literature in envelopes while she worked at the post office so she could spread the word about the fantastic movement that she was part of. She didn't want to miss an opportunity to spread the word about her vision. Just like some BIG visions, she didn't see it happen in her lifetime. But fourteen years after her death, women were granted the right to vote.

When you're fully living in your vision, people might actually think you're a little crazy. Thomas Edison is one of our world's great visionaries who people thought was crazy. Edison acquired a record 1,093 patents. At one time he ran an "invention factory," where he paid others to conduct experiments to turn his dreams into new inventions. As a kid he conducted experiments in his basement. He's known for saying: "Genius is 1 percent inspiration and 99 percent perspiration." He's best known for inventing the electric light system and the system of power plants that make electrical power and the wiring to bring it into people's homes possible.

The cool thing about being a visionary is having the ability to see things before they exist and to sell others on the idea of this thing or service even before it's brought to life. Visionaries do that with one key word—enthusiasm. My vision brought this book to life. My vision sold people on the idea of being involved with this book so much so that several sponsors stepped forward and said I had a pretty cool idea and invested with me to make my vision a reality.

The challenging part about continuously living in your vision as you achieve greater levels of child care business success is what you see with your physical eyes. What you see with your eyes limits the possibilities of what you are capable of making happen. If you're like some of my clients when they first start with me, your reality is dictating a whole different experience than the vision you desire to live in. Perhaps you're experiencing lack, you feel lack, other people reaffirm your feelings of lack and validate the thoughts that randomly pop into your head, and you find it impossible to exist on a different plane that allows you to bring your big vision to life. Because that's what you have to do—exist on a whole different plane so you can visualize and expand your vision daily. Yes, I said daily. Every day your vision needs to be expanding, and that's not hard. It just requires a decision and a consistent commitment to fuel your vision.

I tell my clients, "Think about your vision as a living, breathing person. Give your vision a name. Because if your vision were a person, you would never store her in a box or put a thumbtack through her head and post her on the wall. You would, however, feed her and give her sunlight and talk about her and engage with her daily so she becomes a living, dynamic force."

Looking back at my Child Care Business Success Model, think about your vision as the core of your business. It makes everything else function and helps ensure everything is strong. I often compare the core of my Child Care Business Success Model to the core of your body. Your core is your center, your abdominal strength. Could you imagine what your body would look like if your core, your center, was weak?. Think about what would happen if your abdominal muscles were removed from your body. What would your body look like? Pretty flat, right? And how hard would it be to function in life let alone thrive without abs?

Before we get into the amazing stories that are the backbone of this book, I want to share with you what the backbone of your vision is. Any guesses? It's your story! That's right, your story. Stories are the most underutilized way to market your program and motivate your staff. They are powerful. I was recently onsite with one of my clients, Deidre Nordel, and her team in California. I guided Deidre through a visioning activity where she created a vision that she was connected to, based on the stories that are uniquely and genuinely hers. We were even able to identify her core values from the process. But as we progressed through the day with her entire team, they became charged up and on fire and truly passionate about their child care program. We shot a video and posted it on my Facebook page (**www.facebook.com/childcarebusinesssuccess**), and staff members were raving about our time together and how their energy was totally transformed. If you get a minute, check out the video and see the energy we generated that day with the strategies I'm sharing with you.

I remember Deidre's excitement as we ended the day surrounded by several large pieces of flip-chart paper. When her husband, Steve, showed up to join us for dinner, she grabbed the flip-chart paper with her new vision on it and read it to her husband with authentic excitement for the process we had just gone through. That's what I love about the work I do: being able to take my owners and their entire teams on this transformational journey.

So what's your story, and are you emotionally connected to it? That last question is an incredibly important one. You see, often child care owners are looking to build their lists of how they're different from others. They search for items to add to this list so they can be perceived better than their competition. But the one thing that makes you stand out as being different is the one thing that you just might be hiding. That one thing is YOU and your story. Your story is what sets your program apart from anyone else's child care program. At my annual Child Care Business Success Conference, I have my topic experts (my sponsors) come up on stage and tell their stories. Then what's really interesting for me to see is who my audience connects with based on their stories. When you step up and decide to share yourself and tell your story, you will fill enrollments in record time and attract amazing staff to work for your child care business. You will also come to understand that when you build your vision big and live in that vision and tell your story, there truly is no competition. Because no one else can do YOU like YOU can.

Create as many emotional connection points for you to your business as you can, get really plugged into them and then have conversations with people daily about your vision, and you'll begin to experience transformational results happening. Your enthusiastic words and your authentic and genuine feelings behind them will sell your program.

One of my clients, Gerry, made a wise observation. He said, "Julie, if we could just get everyone on fire and selling the program with enthusiasm, we wouldn't need marketing brochures and all of that other stuff. People would be drawn to us and our programs would be filled." This is truth.

In the upcoming chapters you'll be able to read the transcripts from my interviews—edited and condensed—with several child care business owners who've accomplished amazing things. Please note that these interviews were recorded late 2012 through early 2013. Circumstances for some of our owners have changed; when possible, we've included an update at the end of the chapters.

This book is the first of its kind for child care owners and directors. You'll get to read child care owners' stories. They share mindset shifts, success strategies and details of where they started. As an added bonus, you can tune into the audio recordings of the full interviews and download the full transcripts at **www.ChildCareBusinessSuccessBookVault.com**. The password is **RockMyChildCare.com**.

Chapter 2

Why There Really Is No Competition

Featuring Bill Grant and Timothy O'Shea,
Hildebrandt Learning Centers

"The one thing that you have that nobody else has is you. Your voice, your mind, your story, your vision. So write and draw and build and play and dance and live as only you can."

Neil Gaiman

From the very first time I interacted with Hildebrandt Learning Centers, they stood out in my mind as a company that was really setting the tone for what a successful child care business feels like. That's right, I said *feels like*. Not what they look like or how fancy their marketing brochures are. So why is the word *feel* so important? It's because regardless of what we think, people buy from you based on how they feel in your presence, not on logic. They may justify their decision with points of logic, but it still boils down to emotion. If the energy in your program is good, you will stand out in your community and your enrollments will be high. Parents will just feel something different when they're in your child care program. That's the kind of energy I felt from Hildebrandt many years ago when Leanne Grace, a treasured employee who recently passed away, contacted me to chat about staff motivation. Since then, I've been following them to see what they're doing that generates this contagious type of energy.

The founder of Hildebrant Learning Centers, Bill Grant, has put into practice many success strategies that have led the centers to be on Child Care Information Exchange's top fifty list of North America's largest for-profit child care organizations repeatedly. One of the biggest strategies that you'll discover in my interview with Bill is that he tuned in to his desires of what he wanted to create. When he stuck to those desires and followed his vision, his business model worked. When he didn't, he found that his happiness as a business owner dwindled.

It all started with a desire to create something that didn't exist. Holding accounting and economics degrees as well as an MBA, Bill was working as a controller for a company that served hospitals and nursing homes throughout the country. There was a severe nursing shortage at the time, and Bill suggested to his boss that offering child care on hospital grounds might be a draw to get more nurses. When his boss didn't jump at the idea, Bill stayed in tune with his desire and developed it himself, and guess what? His idea worked!

The first Magic Years Child Care Center was built near a hospital in 1982, and the company grew quickly. After less than a year of operation, the company went public under the Nasdaq symbol KIDS. In five years the company grew from one center to about fifty. Approximately twenty-five to thirty of those were related to hospitals. His idea of creating a "niche" within the child care industry worked beautifully.

While going public was good for investors and shareholders, it didn't sit well with Bill and what he wanted the centers to be. Investors were interested in the bottom line and growth financially, but Bill's desire was to achieve quality in early childhood education. So in 1989 Bill decided to leave the first company he started, which at the time had approximately thirty million dollars in revenue, and which *Inc.* magazine listed as one of the fastest-growing companies in the country.

After sitting out a year to honor a noncompete clause, Bill just couldn't stay away from the business any longer. He was eager to try out his new idea. His idea was to provide high-quality child care structured under a management fee basis, so that the company could concentrate on the quality. Fortunately, his wife, Mary Lou, grew to be just as enthusiastic, and today she is the company's registered dietitian.

Even though Bill Grant can now say that he founded two multimillion-dollar companies, Hildebrandt Learning Centers had meager beginnings in the basement of Bill's home in Pennsylvania in 1991. Bill's wife often clipped coupons and bought day-old bread to make ends meet. Today the company operates forty-five employer- or organization-sponsored early learning programs and two centers that offer adult day services.

The company's high standards and growth didn't just happen by luck or happenstance. I learned the company's story through a private question-and-answer session with Bill and his chief development officer, Timothy O'Shea. Read on as their story unfolds and they share their success strategies for setting yourself apart from all other child care programs in your area. You'll discover exactly how Bill went from the basement of his home to having the fourth-largest employer-sponsored child care management organization in the country.

Julie: Let me just first ask you, what is it about Hildebrandt that makes you guys so special? If a parent was coming in to tour your program, what would you tell the parent about your program?

Bill: Well, I think one of the things that makes us a little bit different than maybe the average child care center is that most of our centers are connected with a sponsor, they're employer-related. So, many of our families that enroll their children, of course, are either working for the company, the state or local agency, or the college or university that we're associated with. One of the things that I think we take on, being related to a sponsor, is the sponsor's culture. Not only is the culture of Hildebrandt in the centers, but so is the culture of the sponsor.

I'll give you a quick example. With Rodale Incorporated, which publishes magazines including *Prevention* and *Organic Gardening*, all of the food that is provided to the children is organic. Also, all of our centers, from a financial standpoint, are built around a cost-plus management fee, so our company receives only a management fee for operating the child care center. That gives our sponsors the ability to decide where they want their child care rates, what time they open and close and what configuration they want for programs before and after school. It gives our clients relief from worrying about day-to-day operations but still providing quality care for their employees and also, in a lot of cases, for the community. One other thing that we're very proud of is that one of the things we do on all of our contracts is require accreditation through NAEYC (National Association for the Education of Young Children). As of July 2013, twenty-nine of our thirty-four early learning centers were accredited by NAEYC.

Julie: That's an amazing accomplishment.

Julie: When we think about a regular child care program, we think about a parent going in for a tour and signing up for a spot, enrolling the child. So how is it different when it comes to employer-sponsored child care?

Tim: What I think is a great piece about it, if you think about working moms or even families going back to work, you have all those challenges. I have a three-week-old son at home.

Julie: Congratulations!

Tim: Thank you very much. But you're going back into the workplace, and you're balancing all those demands, that work-life balance piece, right? So, you've got these families that are at work, and then they're able to go downstairs and visit their children on breaks, at lunchtime. So that whole culture and dynamic really does change the center.

What we enjoy is that we become a partner and a part of the culture of that organization. I think that's really interesting. There is no cookie-cutter Hildebrandt Learning Center. You can walk out to any one of our early learning programs, and it feels completely different from any other. Is there an overriding vision and mission for Hildebrandt Learning Centers? Of course there is. We really focus on providing high-quality programs. The fact is they all represent the communities, the families and our sponsors, and take on their own unique character.

Julie: So do you have a whole team on board who helps customize the experience that each employer is going to have with your program?

Bill: Absolutely.

Julie: Because that's a customization process in itself to say, "Okay, here we go. For this company, this is how we're going to structure it." You have to have some brilliance behind that.

Bill: Well, it's interesting. Tim and I really are the first guys out of the box meeting with companies, listening to hear exactly what they're interested in, developing the needs-assessment surveys, coming back to them and saying, "Here's what we see is the need. This is how much space you would need to accommodate that need. Here's a configuration that might work." The client or the sponsor may tell us, as we're developing the center, do they want their center to break even? Are they willing to subsidize it? With all of that information that Tim and I get, we develop the plan for the child care center and go back to our sponsor to explain exactly what we're going to do. Then our sponsors decide yea or nay, if we're going to go forward with this or table it.

Once we get all of that finished, and if they pull the trigger and say, "We're ready to go," we let Tim go with developing the space plan and the functional plan of what the facility may look like. I start to bring in the other parts of our team—our chief operating officer, our district people and some of our other people from the programs department—to start work on the development of what the center might look like from the standpoint of the program: infants, toddlers, preschoolers, kindergartners, whatever we decide. So yeah, it is a whole team effort. We get involved early on, and our management people get involved with the center early on. As we're going through that process—for, in some cases, up to two years—the sponsor gets to know us, we get to know them and we get a really good feel for exactly what the center is going to look like.

Tim: Bill, I think when you and I consider the growth of the company, and we're looking at where we go and who we're going to partner with, one of the challenges is distance. We now operate centers in West Virginia and New Jersey, but the bulk of them are in

Pennsylvania. We provide such a hands-on approach for our team, to be involved, to help them, that customization. We really are very careful, thoughtful, on where we do expand and how we expand, to ensure that we provide a high-quality program that we can be proud of and that also meets our clients' demands.

Julie: Fantastic. What is your approach when it comes to hiring staff? You have all these locations, many distances between you and them. How do you make sure that the people you are bringing on board are quality and going to be in line with your vision?

Strategy 1

Our only asset, our most important asset, is our staff.

Tim: We just explained to you kind of how Hildebrandt is structured and how we do things. The facilities, we don't own them; they're our sponsors'. You hear this from a lot of companies, but it is true in our case: Our only asset, our most important asset, is our employees. Through that process we've worked to develop systems, and we've got the systems and the job application systems to allow the potential candidates to apply online. Within the first day of hire, they're going in and they get to understand that Hildebrandt wasn't always the company that it is today. Bill started this company twenty-two years ago in his basement, and it's continually grown, based upon his vision, to what it is today. It's important for new employees to understand that and to tie back to that, so that they understand the company that they're working for. Our desire as a company is to continue to provide successful, high-quality programs. I think all those things are important to maintaining that culture. I think any company would say this, that these days, and probably well into the future, one of the biggest challenges will continue to be finding good employees so that you can continue to maintain the culture of the company as it continues to grow.

Julie: I'm always intrigued by where people find employees. I know you have a large program and many people probably looking for employees to fill all of the different positions that open up with Hildebrandt. Is there one person that pops out in mind where you think, "Wow, I can't believe that we found an employee here, and this is a stellar person to work for our team"? A lot of times people feel they're limited by the help-wanted ads or Craigslist or this or that. I hear some really incredible stories about people meeting somebody on an airplane. So I'm just wondering if there's anything like that that pops out for you with all the people you've had to hire.

Tim: I do think it's interesting where we do have families who end up going back to school and work for us at some locations. Globally as a company, we've seen a drastic shift away from paper-based advertisements. If you think about the demographic, everybody's going online and looking for different things, looking at job boards like CareerBuilder. We use a product called Hyrell to advertise, to get the word out about the company, but it also provides us a platform to really talk about Hildebrandt and the programs that we offer.

Bill: We have individuals who work for us now who were in our preschool class eighteen, twenty-one years ago. When I went into one center not too long ago, I was introduced to a young lady. The director said, "I want you to meet one of our new employees." I went over, and she said, "I've known Hildebrandt for a lot of years." I asked, "Really, how's that?" She said, "I was a three-year-old in this classroom." She actually had attended the same center when she was a preschool child, from ages three to five. She had gone through school and college, and then came back and works for us.

Julie: When people put that on their résumé, that they attended preschool at Hildebrandt, does that give them a competitive edge?

Bill: Absolutely.

Tim: That's actually the first part of the job application, where you went to preschool.

Bill: We've had opportunities in Arizona, Indiana, Texas and so forth. They look interesting, with very large companies, colleges or universities. But we were able to hold back on that and say, "No, we're not going to do that." If we move to an area in western Pennsylvania, people know of us. They know we're at this college or this company and have heard a lot of good things about our organization. It's important also for us not just to operate child care centers, but also to get the word out to everyone in our profession about quality child care. We use a lot of our people, who are excellent people, from our behavioral specialists to our chief operations officer who does a lot of training. We're out there in our communities and throughout the states doing some of those trainings, getting ourselves known, and people associate us with that quality. We're a known product when we go into a lot of areas, so that's also a plus for us to get employees to apply.

Tim: On top of that, we really do focus, and we strive to provide the best wages that we can to our employees. We try to increase the benefits packages, all-encompassing. The early childhood industry is not a high-income industry, so we strive to set the bar and push those wages and benefits as far ahead as we possibly can. The structure of our company allows us to work with our clients or sponsoring organizations to be able to do that.

Julie: Do you guys do anything creative when it comes to your employee communication? We always have people who are like, "Oh, gosh, we can never get together for staff meetings." Is there anything you do that you think is just really cutting edge when it comes to communicating with employees?

Tim: I don't know if it's cutting edge, but we do Touching Minds on Mondays. We send out companywide communications to folks, coaching and mentoring newsletters every month, things along those lines to really communicate. Again, it reinforces the culture of the company when you get messages from folks like Bill and myself and Judy.

Bill: One of the other things we've developed for training, which we think is really great, we call "napinars." During naptime when children may be sleeping, staff can pull up their laptops, which we have provided in the classrooms. We have trainings that are online that our professional development people create. Some are interactive. Some are already stored. Staff are given a reading prior to the napinar. Then the napinar may be twenty minutes to a half-hour long. Then afterward they do a project of understanding to make sure they understand exactly what they're doing and start to implement with photos and so forth to show they understand what was happening. Then they give it to our director of professional development to make sure they understood what was going on. That also gives them training credits they need.

On top of that, we want our staff to have time with their families so they don't have to go out in the evenings or on Saturdays to get some additional training. Some do, of course. Napinars are only one piece of that training process. Our average person is getting twenty-four to twenty-eight hours of training per year, on top of CPR and first aid and medication administration and so forth. It's probably closer to forty hours. We try to respect the fact that our employees have families also. We came up with this a couple of years ago, and it's been a real success. The employees love it. It's nice because we can do that training that our centers really need. It's not just some topic out there that someone is doing at a local college. If it's something that our centers are in need of specifically, we can design that specifically for our needs. It's been a big success.

Tim: Right now that's only done in-house. We have considered looking at other ways to promote those things out to a larger community.

Julie: Tim, you were saying that it's really important to get staff on board with the vision right from the start, from the orientation process. I really heard passion coming through your voice. How did you get started, especially being a man, in child care? A lot of times we hear women say, "Oh, well, I had children and didn't like the child care programs around me." To have a man come into the picture and establish what you did is incredible.

Bill: It is interesting. When I look at the demographics of our employees—we run around 1,000 employees now—we probably have a dozen men, if we're lucky.

People always ask me, "How did you get the name Hildebrandt?" We were sitting around the table at the lawyer's office, throwing out names. They were calling to check, and this was taken and that was taken. Finally the lawyer turned to me. "Bill, what road do you live on?" I said, "Hildebrandt Road." He said, "Hey, how about Hildebrandt Learning Centers?" I said, "That's a catchy name." My business cards for the first couple of years was for Hildebrandt Learning Centers, Hildebrandt Road in Dallas, Pennsylvania. As I was going into hospitals and visiting other clients, they were seeing this company had a road named after it! They just thought I was this huge company. I was able to start getting some clients and grew to somewhere around twenty to twenty-four clients.

In 1998, '99, a bigger company that's still out there decided to come and ask me if I would be a part of their organization. I listened to them, and what they wanted to do, and about quality and being the greatest child care center in the world. I went along with them. For about a year and a half, we were part of another, larger company. After about six or seven months, we realized the idea was not quality. It was back to the same thing about profitability and growth. I went back to the principals of that company and asked to have my company back. They were hesitant at first, but after a couple of hours of convincing them, they gave me my company back. I made two mistakes in my life: one, going public, and two, joining forces with someone else. I told myself I would not do that again. I would grow and do quality centers and accreditations and so forth. That's what we've been doing ever since.

Strategy 2

When it's a family affair, driven by passion, no one is a clock-watcher.

The nice thing about being a privately held company and a family business is that we're not pressured to grow two centers, three centers, add profits to the bottom line. It's interesting, because the way I think sometimes is, if we get a new center, the first thing I do is usually go to my program and curriculum department and say, "We have a new center. We're going to get a little bit more in management fees. What else do we need to do?" Whether that's hiring a behavior specialist or someone else, we use our dollars to make sure we enhance the qualities of the program. That's the nice thing about being a family business. Hopefully we'll always keep it that way, as long as I'm here. I'm not sure what happens with the next generation with Tim and Lauren, because they're very much interested in staying with the company.

Julie: This is a family affair, right?

Tim: Bill works two doors down from me. My wife works across the hall. His sister works up at the front desk at purchasing. Bill's wife, Mary Lou, is the registered dietitian within the company. Six years ago, Lauren and I were both living in Philadelphia. Bill came to us and was gauging our interest. Lauren was very passionate. Hildebrandt has been a part of her entire life. As we were talking and looking at different opportunities, Bill's vision really sold me on coming on board with Hildebrandt. When I realized the breadth of clients they had, the quality of programs, when I started going and seeing them firsthand, I realized how special Hildebrandt was.

Both Lauren and myself left our jobs in Philadelphia and moved here and joined forces with Bill. Luckily enough, over the past couple of years, we've been very successful, even in a down economy. We've been very lucky to continue to grow. I say *lucky*, but I really don't believe it. I think it's Bill. The way he set up this company, he set it up for success. We're all committed to that same vision of providing quality care. We get people calling us and begging us to operate centers on their behalf. When you're in a position like that and you have a product that's in demand, I think it helps and enables you to be successful going forward. It's been pretty amazing. I was talking to our payroll specialist a couple of days ago. In six years, we've close to doubled the number of people we pay. While we've not doubled the number of centers we operate, a lot of our newer centers are a lot larger than the original centers. With all that comes all the other demands of more staff and managing that. It's been an interesting transformation from a smaller company to a medium-sized organization over the past couple of years, and still maintaining that feel. We're not a big, corporate entity. We're a family business. Our focus is on providing the most for our employees and for the children and families we serve.

Julie: Were there a lot of fears that came up when you thought, *We're going to go and work with Dad*? What were some of those closed-door conversations about that? There are a lot of programs, small and large, that operate with that family dynamic. What were some of your concerns?

Tim: It is completely different. For anybody that thinks it doesn't bring other things into the mix, they're mistaken. There are tons of benefits, and they definitely outweigh any challenges we face. One of the biggest concerns was for Lauren and myself working side by side every day. We didn't want it to affect our marriage or have work come home with us and burden us. I do have to say we're all very respectful. We try not to bring things home. We try not to carry it through the weekends. Of course, those conversations do occur. We had some conversations right from the get-go that enabled us to be able to work successfully together. I think it's been a great partnership over the last six years for us.

Bill: I agree. Six or seven years ago, before Tim and Lauren came up here, I talked about, "Gee, I don't know what I'm going to do going forward. We're getting to be a bigger company. There are more demands. Maybe what we need to do is join forces with another company or sell the company." I remember Lauren getting very upset about that, saying, "Dad, this is something we've been involved with. I was three years old and cutting the ribbons to new centers, playing with the toys." I said, "You're right." I thought about that. I saw in her eyes that she really wanted to be a part of this going forward, and that made me feel really good. Early on, we would talk about things, like Tim said, on the weekends and so forth. We finally just made a rule and said, "Look, if we don't *have* to talk about the business, let's forget about it." We've done very well with that plan. It's been a good run and success. We continue to grow. We look at what we have, even in the pipeline now, and we smile knowing we have organizations that contact us that want child care centers. We're still very busy, which is great.

Julie: That's fantastic. Again, I can hear the passion in your voice. When you're an entrepreneur, it's almost like your business is your life, right?

Bill: It is.

Julie: Sometimes it makes it fun when you have all those boundaries and guidelines in place, to keep certain communication out of our personal lives.

Bill: It is. The nice thing I see with Tim and Lauren and a lot of other individuals is that no one here is a clock-watcher. It's, "What do we have to do to get the job done, to be the best?" That really makes me feel good, that people are that committed to providing quality care for children. They really work very hard. We have great people working for us. It's not just Bill or Tim or Lauren. We're the quarterbacks trying to get everybody going, but we have some really, really great, talented people. I don't know where I'd be without them, quite frankly.

Strategy 3
The fire in your eyes will set you apart.

Julie: Bill, when you think about being an entrepreneur and your favorite part of the day, or what you love doing most, what would that be? What do you think it is with this entity that you created that brings you the most joy?

Bill: I really enjoy going out and meeting new clients, both new clients and the clients we actually have had for the last twenty-two or so years. I'm not a salesman, although a lot of people say I'm pretty good at doing that. I believe in our program, and I believe in what we're doing. I can't tell you the client's name that I'm going to say this about, because a contract is not signed yet, but it's a very prestigious client. When we did our presentation a couple of years ago, when the first go-round happened, there were something like fifteen organizations that made presentations to this organization. I can remember walking into the building, and representatives from one of the companies that had just presented before me were walking out. They had five people, carrying all kinds of screens and cameras and everything else. I walked in with Judy Witmer, our chief operating officer, just ourselves with some printed materials. We sat down for three hours and talked about what we do, what we believe in, how we want to approach this and so forth. We left, and I said, "That was a good experience. We'll see what happens."

A couple of weeks later, we got a telephone call from the human resources director, who said, "Bill, we've chosen your company to be the provider for child care." I almost fell off my seat. I said, "Really!?" I said to her, "What got us up to the top?" She said, "We believe in you and the passion. This was not just a job or a business to you. This is a part of your life." That made it very visible to these individuals, and that's why they chose us. I think we approach every center that way, whether they're the biggest organization I just spoke about or school districts that just want to add school-age programs. People believe in us. They see that we're passionate about what we're doing. That's really our success.

Julie: They see it in your eyes and they hear it in your voice.

Bill: They do.

Julie: That's really powerful. I think that's a big part of staff motivation, which is what I've been teaching for thirteen years in this industry. Tim, I'm wondering, when you have new employees on board, what is it and how is it that you communicate to them who Hildebrandt is? Maybe you can give us a little sample of that. I'm getting a tinge of that during this interview, but I think that you bring it out in a very powerful way when you talk to employees. I would love to hear how that goes down.

Tim: Julie, to be honest with you, we try to capture what Bill just said. When you hear his story, it tells you a lot about his learning experience and how it molded what Hildebrandt is today. What we try to do is capture that in a nutshell. There are a lot of employees, and distance between centers, but we've developed a presentation that really summarizes the message of what we are as a company. I think that carries through. We have a lot of longtime staff, a lot of longtime directors. When those folks are interacting with these new employees, I think that carries the same message. It starts with Bill, but it carries all the way through the organization. I think it's something that's pretty interesting. We did this a couple of years back. In all the center directors' offices, it says, "Is it in the best interest of the children and families?" If you base your decisions off that, you're probably making the right choice. When you have a culture that really is focused on providing and looking for ways to support families, provide them high-quality care, I think it just becomes a pervasive thing across the company. The new employees quickly learn what it is and what we're about as an organization.

Strategy 4
Don't hide.

Bill: Tim and I are not suit-and-tie guys behind desks all day. We're out in the centers, visiting, talking with staff. I can remember when we were opening up one center, we were in our shorts and T-shirts, sweating, opening up boxes and doing things. I remember a new staff person who didn't know me yet saying something to the director. I'm doing all this and she was giving me orders. The director almost fell over and said, "Oh, my God, do you realize he's the CEO of the company?" She kept apologizing to me.

We get involved with the centers. People see us doing things. How can you run a business without knowing what's going on in your centers and seeing and touching and feeling from the beginning of the center right through the opening? That's important. When we open centers and start training, we're the first people there. We talk about our company and the culture and what we expect. They see us first before they actually get into all the program and curriculum people and all the training. They get to know us. We have many employees who've been with me fifteen, twenty, twenty-two years. I know their families. I know where their kids are. I know what colleges they've graduated from. It gets harder with 1,000 employees, but I walk into the centers and it's, "Hi, Bill, how are you?" That's important. We talk about being a family business. We truly look at all of our employees as part of our family. One of the things we do, we have a company picnic every year, which not many companies have anymore. This year I think 1,200 people attended.

Tim: Yeah, a little over 1,200 people came. It's employees and their families.

Bill: That's the way we look at it. We want everybody to understand that we are a family. We're working together. We're not this big organization, this big corporation that has a bunch of shareholders and so forth. We try to do the right thing for kids and families. I think most people in our company get that message. They really do get that message from us.

Strategy 5
Stick to your guns.

Julie: I think that's what a lot of entrepreneurs lose sometimes, their vision and their passion for what they're doing. Sometimes it's because of being swayed by a parent who wants this or someone who wants that. They're working really hard to try to make their business model work. What do you guys say to those people who are like, "It's so easy for me to lose my vision, because I want to make everybody happy who comes in wanting child care. They come in and want my service, but I feel I need to move this way and that way, change this, do that."

Bill: I think any individual thinking about being in early childhood needs to stick to their guns. There have been times when a potential client has come to us and we've turned them down. We've turned down business and walked away from what could be lucrative clients. Their vision and what they wanted to do didn't align with what we're doing. If you stay true to your principles, you'll find that, over the long run, it's going to be successful. If you start to chip away at the things you believe in and start to give up those kinds of things, you may grow and be a little more financially better off—

Tim: In the short term.

Bill: Yeah, in the short term. Can you sleep at night? That's the thing. I go home every night and I keep saying to myself, *I know I'm doing something good for kids and families.* There is nothing that we're doing in this company that I would say is not in the best interest of kids and families. That makes me feel good. All of our management people think that way. Tim thinks that way. My four-year-old granddaughter is in one of our centers. I need to make sure that those centers are great. I have family in those centers. That's important. That's what I would tell individuals who are thinking about getting into this business or are already in this business. Tim and I talked about this. When he first came on, we were going from being that small company, as Tim said, maybe five hundred employees to 1,000, from twenty-two centers to forty-three centers. Are we going to lose that vision and mission that we've always said we set out to do? We have not. We're the same company, from the standpoint that our principles are today as they were six years ago and maybe ten years ago.

Julie: Was there ever a point when you felt scared that your model or what you were creating wasn't going to work, that you weren't going to get the clients, that the money wasn't going to come in? Was there ever a moment for you? If so, how did you overcome that?

Strategy 6
Stand in confidence and forget the competition.

Bill: I have to admit, when I talked to my wife about leaving the company that I had started and starting Hildebrandt, we had no clients, but I was confident there were enough companies and individuals and organizations in Pennsylvania where we started that would listen to my story and believe in what we believed in, and I wanted to do the best for our employees. I knew we were going to get clients. I wasn't sure if we were going to have two or five or ten the first year, but I knew there were people out there who were going to come with us. I really wasn't scared at that point. Was it tough for the first couple of years? Sure was. For the first nine or ten months, I had no salary at all. My wife was looking in Sunday papers to clip coupons. She'd go to the day-old-bread store to buy bread to make ends meet. It was tough at first. I had the support of my wife and my children. Lauren, at that point, was very young, but I think she knew what was going on. I had that support. If you have that kind of support, I think you can go out and be successful. I wasn't scared.

Julie: Fantastic. What I hear from you is that you built your business around a desire in your heart. You had a big vision. With a desire in our hearts, I think we always view competition differently. Do you think, for what you do, there is competition? Do you not worry about the competition?

Bill: I think there is competition for what we do as a business. Do I think there's competition out there for how we provide? I don't. I believe we do something that is a niche, that's a little different than the bigger companies out there doing this. I don't worry about competition. It's not like we're going over websites every couple of days of the bigger companies out there. Families and clients really give us credit for what we do, so why should we change anything we're doing? We change what's going on in the industry, maybe from the standpoint of program and curriculum. That's always changing, of course. But from the standpoint of where our ideas are and what we're doing, we change very little.

Tim: I'd say the biggest difference we've made in recent years is the way we market to families. I think what we previously did, somewhat of a disservice to ourselves, was we relied a lot on word of mouth. Now we're realizing and trying to, I hate to say "promote" or "market" the company, but really getting the word out about what's happening in the programs, how our programs are so drastically different than what else is out there. Trying to get families to come in and see the difference has been our biggest thing. It's not so much that we're changing what we're doing. We're trying to get the word out there to more individuals so that they *know* what we're doing.

Julie: So you're being seen as a big presence.

Tim: Right. Again, it's kind of a catch-22. You don't want to be seen as a big entity, but you want people to understand what you do and how many clients you have, how successful you are, but at the same time that you are really focusing on the center level.

Julie: What is your strategy for advertising? Word of mouth, of course, has been a big thing for you. What are you doing now that's going to help you have a bigger effect?

Tim: You think about the demographic. Not too long ago, within six years, predominately we were using a lot of paper-based advertisements. That's drastically shifted over to the Web. That goes through all different sorts of formats, whether it's Google AdWords or geo-targeting, marketing campaigns online, banner ads, all sorts of different things you try to do. We really do see that most folks these days are going to the Internet to try to find out about the company or checking reviews, going to social media, Facebook, Twitter. Pinterest is now a big one women are going to.

Strategy 7
Surround yourself with good people.

Julie: As two gentlemen in the child care industry, what is your best advice to other men in the industry, whether they're thinking about owning their own programs or even teaching in programs? I know there are a lot of concerns that come up.

Tim: My wife is great. Like Bill mentioned earlier, we work with a lot of women who came to this industry a long time ago, but their passions lie in the same realm as Bill's and my own. Surround yourself with a good group of people, women or men. If they're focused on quality early childhood education, you're going to surround yourself with the right folks.

Bill: It's interesting from a management level. I've heard clients say to me that because we are men, when we come in we have a better handle on the financial part, the business part. I think there are very, very competent females in this business who probably could run circles around me and Tim. On the center level, you don't see that many males going into the centers. I'm sure you probably know that. That's unfortunate. We find that when we hire college students for our summer programs, juniors or seniors in college. The kids really gravitate toward those males. Some children unfortunately just don't have a male figure in their lives. It would be nice if we could get a couple of more males. We probably have two dozen males, but it's a very, very tiny percentage of the caregivers we have.

Tim: The ones we do have are awesome.

Julie: I hear that in every child care program I go in and work with. They love the men. For some reason it seems men are hesitant to get in. They're worried, concerned.

Tim: I think it's a combination of both society as it is today and some reservations on the gentlemen's part.

Bill: Also, I think the wage levels that unfortunately come with child care. . . . This is especially a problem if the male is supposed to be the wage earner for the family. I don't know what the average wage is these days in child care. I think it's something around $12 an hour. As I said, males come into the business with lower wages and limited benefits. That may be one reason we don't get as many males in the industry. That's unfortunate. I'm hoping that, over the years, that changes and our clients see the importance of early childhood and give us more and more dollars to work with so we can pay those individuals to get good, quality people in the centers.

Tim: Clients, families, society, government, all those avenues.

Strategy 8

Remember your why.

Julie: What do you think is the absolute best thing about starting a child care business? If you could look back and say, "This is the best thing in the world," what would you say is the best thing about it?

Bill: I'm sitting in my office. I'm looking at a bookshelf, on the bottom level, probably two feet high, three rows over, of letters, comments, e-mails, cards from families, kids and so forth, who have said great things, employees also, just great things about our company and what we do and how we've changed their lives. For me, we're a success doing that. I've already put some of those into a box, so that when I'm a little older, I can pull those out. That, to me, is success. It's not financial; it's what we're doing for kids and families. I look at these kids, and I even look at my granddaughter. They're the future of our country, our future leaders and citizens and employees. We've got to give these kids a good start. There's enough research out there that says by age five, 90 percent of a child's brain development happens. How important it is to have a good, quality program. That's going to be the difference in this country, if we can give all children, not just the children in Hildebrandt, but every child, a good, high-quality program and a good start in life. That's important.

Tim: I was along the same lines. My life changed almost four years ago when my daughter was born. She was in one of our programs for the first couple of years of her life. I take such pride in what our teachers do. When she comes home at the end of the day, the things she learns, it amazes me, but reinforces the importance of what we do every day. There are 2,500-plus families, 4,500 kids, coming in and out of the centers every day. They're all receiving that same quality education. It does bring a smile to your face and is something to be proud of.

Julie: What do you think is the biggest challenge you overcame?

Tim: I guess for me it was managing the growth of the company, the fact that we evolved from doing three or four or five centers, thinking you have a handle on every little thing. I was involved in everything, from the standpoint of financial and programming and so forth. Then it moved to the next level. You'd get away from certain pieces of it. I think that's probably the biggest challenge. I don't have my finger in every single thing in the company. From the standpoint of 10,000 feet, I'm looking over at some of these items. I miss that a little. With forty-three centers, you can't get to every center every month. I miss that part. I think the challenge is moving from a small to medium-sized company. That transition was probably the biggest challenge for me.

Strategy 9
Let go to grow.

I'd argue that we're still going through that transition. I keep thinking, *Is there going to be that one day when we're all done and have successfully made the transition?* I don't think there will ever be that day. It will constantly change. Keep that vision in mind, and focus on that. When change does happen, making sure it aligns with that vision is really important for us as we continue to grow.

Julie: It goes back to you have to let go to grow, right?

Bill: You do. One of the things I think Tim has brought is moving this from the standpoint of technology, giving our directors the tools to be better managers, to be able to spend more time in classrooms and with children and parents and staff. They're not pushing papers in an office. Tim has done a great job over the last five years doing that. Some of the technology I don't even understand, but I know everybody who's using it loves it. That's been a big plus for us too.

Tim: My view of technology and how it plays a role for the company—we're not always trying to grab the newest thing out there, to have the best, newest software. There's one thing you can't buy more of, and that's time, for every one of us. There comes a point when you have to consider how you can leverage technology to work smarter, better, more efficiently, and really get our highest-paid, highest-educated folks—whether they be the directors or regional folks or program specialists in the center—away from data entry, away from computers as much as possible, and really focusing on the children and families. I really think that's where technology is. How we view it as a company has really helped us be more efficient in what we do.

Julie: That's powerful. I think getting out from behind the computer is really important, especially when you're looking to grow.

Tim: It's a fine balance.

Julie: We talked about having a public partnership. Is there anything else you'd identify that you'd really do differently, if you had the opportunity to?

Bill: I don't have anything I would do differently. I get up every morning and get here earlier and earlier every day. I think today I was here at ten after six. It's been fun for me. There have been challenges, little things that happen from day to day. I don't think I'd change anything. If I had to go back in time and do it all over again, I would do it exactly the way I did it.

Julie: Tim, is there anything you could think of that you would do differently in the role that you've had or responsibilities?

Tim: I also have been pretty pleased with what's happened in my time here. I think we've really been able to continue to grow and really maintain the company vision and values.

Julie: What about things you would do more of? We talked about leveraging time. If time wasn't an issue, is there something you feel you would do more of to grow your company or just to make it more what you want?

Strategy 10
Provide high-quality child care for all.

Bill: For me, I just want to add onto what Tim was talking about with marketing. Many of our clients, of course, are closed centers, and only their employees can use them. Some enroll from the community at large. I would just like families to be able to come into our centers, take a look, evaluate what quality is. Even if they can't get into one of our centers and have to go to another center, I'd like them to push those other centers to be high quality. As I said, our goal in our company is not just to provide high quality for our 4,500 kids. It's to provide high quality for every child that we possibly can, every family we touch, every tour we do, to make sure they understand the high quality. Maybe we have a waiting list in that infant room and you have to stay in your current center, but go back and tell people what you see and push people to be their best.

Tim: Raise the bar.

Bill: That's what we've always talked about. That's really important to us.

Julie: That's for all child care programs, not just yours, you're saying?

Bill: That's right.

Julie: That's a critical shift in mindset. A lot of people are focusing on the competition, but you're saying you want it for everybody.

Bill: That's correct. It makes it good for everybody in this industry. The problem is that I think many people look at child care and early learning centers as day care. Our staff aren't considered, in many cases, as professionals. They're looked at as day care, low-paid workers. We've got to keep raising that bar. We have to have our families

45

look at somebody who has either a two- or four-year degree and re-alize that they spent the time, got the education, know what's best for your child. That's important. We have to continue to raise the bar. If we as a profession want everyone out there to look at us as a true profession, we have to work on it. It's not just Hildebrandt. It's every single center. The mom-and-pop down the street, if they need help on something, we have no problem helping them. If we have train-ings, we invite people to our trainings. In Pennsylvania, there's the Pennsylvania Child Care Association. Tim is doing training through that group on how to design natural playgrounds. Other people in our company are training in other areas. We share that information. We don't just keep it to ourselves, and that's important.

Update: Hildebrandt Learning Centers was acquired by Bright Horizons Family Solutions in 2015.

To hear this interview in its entirety, go to **www.ChildCareBusinessSuccess BookVault.com**. The password is **RockMyChildCare.com**.

Chapter 3

Customer and Staff Loyalty

Featuring Vernon Mason, Jr., Wee School Child Development Centers

"People complain when there is too much sun and it gets unbearably hot, and also when it rains too much or when it is cold. But, no one grumbles when the moon shines. Everyone becomes happy and appreciates the moon in their own special way. Children watch their shadows and play in its light, people gather at the square to tell stories and dance through the night. A lot of happy things happen when the moon shines. These are some of the reasons why we should want to be like the moon."

Ishmael Beah

*O*ne thought stands out in my mind about the owner of Wee School Child Development Centers, Vernon Mason, Jr. That one thought is that he is truly a likeable child care leader. This doesn't mean that he strives to be liked, but more that he is naturally liked because of his personality and style of leadership and management. Just like the moon, he shines.

Even when a natural disaster destroyed his child care program in September of 1999, he continued to shine! Hurricane Floyd rushed in, and within a matter of twenty-four hours, Mr. Mason's program was destroyed. Water flooded his child care program, reaching levels higher than the door frames, and remained for days. Everything was destroyed except for his spirit and, now, his inspiring story of child care business success.

Just like the moon, he persevered and reopened the doors to Wee School Child Development the following weekend at its new location. The new school had tables and chairs, but not a single toy or manipulative. The new center was in a rough neighborhood and out of the way from the former location. Vernon knew that if his existing clients did not show up, the company simply wouldn't make it.

But when you're a likeable child care leader, parents and staff remain loyal. Parents showed up with their children, carrying bags of toys that would have put Santa to shame! About sixty children showed up the first day, and the number grew from there. Vernon considers that the biggest compliment he ever received.

Vernon's mother, Nancy, started the company more than thirty years ago so that she could stay at home with her own three children while she cared for other children. After Vernon earned an accounting degree and spent some time in retail, they decided to take her business to an entirely different level. With only a $5,000 credit card, Vernon and his mom opened Ms. Nancy's Child Care together.

As an accounting major, Vernon sat down and created graphs and charts and everything else he could think of to help track the business. Six months into opening the first program, he put all of those into the shredder and started over. Theory and real world often do not align. Mother and son reverted back to Nancy's vision and reputation as their driving force to child care business success and never looked back.

This approach has led to a business that operates in four communities with over eighty staff members caring for more than five hundred children. And Vernon himself is a sought-after speaker, in the business community and at early education conferences across the United States.

Fortunately, you don't have to experience a natural disaster to make the most of your business. Read on to discover more of what Vernon has learned during his years of working in child care and growing Wee School Child Development Centers.

Julie: You're laying out charts and graphs, and then one day you think, *Forget this*, and into the shredder they go. What was that moment of realization when you decided, *This stuff goes into the shredder*? Why did you think that?

Vernon: It probably came along with a few choice words. It's when you realize that the bank account is not keeping up with the theory. In the real world, some people don't always pay. In the real world, you have to pay staff members more than you thought you were going to have to pay. In the real world, benefits cost more than you think they're going to, the overhead is higher. In the real world, you would like to get a paycheck. I can remember going to the bank and cashing my first paycheck. I happened to know the teller. It was $135, and she actually laughed. We had a cordial relationship, but I drove away, thinking, *Wow, that was insulting! She's laughing at my paycheck.* I always had a little vision in the back of my mind. I believed, in some mild visualization, if you build it, they'll come. I always felt like there were bigger things to come. It didn't really bother me.

Strategy 1
Pay yourself.

Julie: This is a common challenge that many owners, many directors, go through, especially ones I enroll in our Money Acceleration Program. They say, "I don't even take a paycheck. If I do, it's minimal. It's less than what my lowest-paid staff member makes."

Vernon: I have done some consultations with other directors. I am president of the North Carolina Licensed Child Care Association, and we give a Director of the Year award. Typically I will go visit the programs of directors who are nominated. I can walk in, having been in the field for more than twenty years, and I can talk to the director for a couple of minutes and say, "You aren't paying yourself, are you?" They're driving a vehicle that the program is paying for, the program is paying the insurance, and most of their groceries the program buys. When it comes to taking a salary home, they pay everybody else, pay the rent, pay the overhead, feed the kids, and then there's nothing left at the end. I think in our field, often we have people who will build those people up, "Oh, my gosh, look at all she does. Look at the work she does." I'm not undermining or demeaning the work that she does, or that the program is doing, but in this formula has got to be compensation for the directors.

Julie: Absolutely. It's a feeling too, I think, that it's really hard to grow a business if there's not a value placed on you and your skills and what you're delivering to the world. It really becomes hard to grow it and be able to step away from it.

Vernon: Absolutely. In turn, that also affects the owners' outlook and pessimism or optimism. It's hard to stay optimistic when you can't pay yourself.

Julie: There are so many conferences I've been to where the theme is, "This is only child care." It's all about budget cuts and how there's not enough, not enough, not enough. That's why with this Child Care Business Success Movement, I really want to shine a light on the success that is possible in this industry, so that we do have that transformation in mindset to bring us to another level with what we're creating.

Vernon: Absolutely. My mom and I, we built this program. Early on I realized my mom was really great with kids, but not so much with supervising staff. About a year and a half into the program, my mom stepped aside and went into a classroom. She remained there until she retired a number of years ago. I took the role of the leadership of the organization. We outgrew the small building and renovated a private school and church in town. We renovated the classrooms first, because that was simplest. We filled those up and then took more than half the sanctuary and put in classrooms and filled that up. I really knew we were making headway when we had to tear out the baptistery. You don't really need a baptistery in a preschool, so we tore out the baptistery to put in more classrooms. We completely filled up that program.

We didn't have the newest building. We didn't have the shiniest vans. We didn't have the best equipment in town. We started on a shoestring. The way we started our program was with a $5,000 credit card I had. We had no backer out there. My family members are not wealthy people at all, so there was no family money to pay our way. It was pay as we go. We really competed against people with much nicer buildings, much fancier, but we were able to hold our own. It can be done. Many people will use the excuse "I can't fill up my program because there's a new center down the road with new equipment and a bright, shiny building."

Julie: It's got heated floors and upgraded playground equipment.

Vernon: Absolutely. It's about the relationships you build with the families and staff. The biggest compliment I ever had, and still to this day, was when our center was destroyed. It was destroyed in Hurricane Floyd. We were in a low-lying area, and a hurricane came in and flooded the building. When I say flooded the building, I don't mean three feet of water in the building, I mean that it went above the door frames of the program and stayed there for three days. There was no salvaging, no walking out with anything. It was all completely gone in a matter of twenty-four hours. We were closed for a couple of days.

Strategy 2
Be worth driving out of the way for.

Over that weekend, I signed a month-to-month lease because I was concerned every night whether we would survive. I knew the staff we had were as invaluable to us as the equipment we had. I knew if we had to close for six months or nine months or a year, the staff wouldn't be there. I just didn't know if I wanted to start over again. I signed a month-to-month rental on a closed program in downtown Wilson, where this program started. We literally had a barbed-wire fence around our playground. Parents drove to downtown Wilson in a rough neighborhood where I had to regularly run the homeless people away from our parents in the parking lot. Those parents drove for a year while our new building was being constructed in the new location. That, to this day, is the biggest compliment I ever received. People always say they choose you for convenience. These parents drove out of their way for a year. It was very heartwarming, very meaningful to us.

Julie: I got chills with you sharing all of that. Incredible what you've overcome. It's incredible that you had the desire so strongly within you that you knew there was more and you knew the direction to take. What do you think helped you build those strong positive relationships with parents? A lot of times it's a fine line between having good boundaries, so you're getting paid on time, and you're not giving parents loans and that kind of thing, with having them being so committed to you. What are the boundaries that you have in place with parents, and what do you think is at the core of those relationships?

Strategy 3
Remember that your business is, well, a business.

Vernon: The core of the relationship is the genuine concern for their families and for their children's well-being, and trying to surround yourself with staff members who feel the same way, who have genuine concern and care for the families. You know that saying, "People will want to be there." That's the best thing. Regarding boundaries, I can tell you I have probably lost as much in accounts receivables as anybody. I have been burned with people. We did excuses, anything from parents saying they spent too much at the grocery store to people who I've gone to in the parking lot and knocked on the BMW and said, "If you don't pay me today, you can't come back tomorrow, and by the way, I like your new car."

Julie: I like that big-screen TV you've got in the backseat.

Vernon: Absolutely. You just have to draw boundaries. Business is business. When I develop a rapport with them, they have to understand that I'm taking off my hat of care and concern for your family and putting on my hat of "we have to pay our bills and staff." If we let you not pay and the next people not pay, we can't do that.

Julie: How important do you think it really is to think of your child care program as a business?

Strategy 4

The big picture requires more time working ON programs and less time working IN them.

Vernon: A local peer in North Carolina who owns about twenty programs said, "Vernon, I have to make my program successful. I have to spend more time working *on* them and less time working *in* them." I think that's a great quote. My role has changed now that I have multiple centers. I don't go into programs every day and stay all day. It's hard to look at the big picture when you're looking for Johnny's pacifier and you're giving the Biting Talk 101: Why Toddlers Bite. I have people who do things like that. I have to spend time on the business side of it. It's one of those things, when you get in this field, you almost have to force yourself. You have to block your time and say, "Tuesday is my office day. I will work on the office, on the business side of things." That's how I'm able to do that.

Julie: So thinking about it as a business is pretty important to you, to be able to grow it?

Vernon: Yes. It goes hand in hand. It's not a greed thing. You have to look at the business side to be successful. You'll never reach success if you ignore the business side.

Strategy 5

Healthy organizations produce healthy children.

Julie: Let's say we take a lot of pride in being a child care business, and we're okay with that and okay with saying that to parents. What do you think that means? When you hear, "We're a successful child care business," what should really resonate in our listeners' ears? What does being a successful business offer to parents?

Vernon: I believe that healthy organizations produce healthy children. I don't believe unhealthy businesses or organizations can produce healthy outcomes for children. When the owners are worried about keeping the lights on, are not able to provide any kind of benefits to the staff, the swinging door is open with staff members coming and going, that's not good for kids. Children typically will not stay in programs like that. The healthier your organization is, I believe the healthier your program is and the better the outcome is for children.

Julie: How do you deal with the heartbreak when you really have a parent or child you want to save? You know they're going through rough times or whatever, not paying their bills. Maybe this is tougher for women business owners. We often hear, "We see the possibility. We see the potential." This applies not only to clientele but also to staff. I think it keeps our businesses stuck. Have you ever had a situation where you felt like, *Man, I just would love to save this family, but I know it'll disempower me as a business owner?*

Vernon: I think what you have to look at is, let's say, giving them a discount or a hold on tuition. If you give them a discount on tuition, or allow them not to pay for a week of tuition, or however you want to phrase that, is this going to fix the situation, or is it just going to make an inevitable situation worse? Have they had something major happen? Has one of the children been hospitalized? Has the parent had to miss work and they didn't get paid? Have they had a lot of money put out for a specific reason in an emergency situation? If it's something like that, you can write off a week or two of tuition, and then they can get back on track. If it's something where everything is the same—they're bad at budgeting money, they can't pay their bill—and if you give them this week free, they'll just pay next week late, then at that point you'll just have to say, "I really would love to help you, but we just can't." The other part of that is, you can't continue dragging it out. If you're going to help a family, help and write it off, no holding grudges, no looking back. You do it and move on and acknowledge it. It's like a hospital. They write off some for people who can't afford hospital bills. In child care, we all have to do that sometimes also.

Julie: How did you develop the name Wee School?

Strategy 6

Set your business up to be sold.

Vernon: Initially when we opened, it was named after my mom, Nancy. It was called Ms. Nancy's Child Care. Locally in town we had a program that sold. It was named after a lady. When it sold, the name went with it. My mother said, "I can't imagine you selling one day and selling my name." I said, "Really? Well, then we need to work on that." My business hat came on, and I told my mother that at the time when we would sell, part of what we would sell would be her reputation and her name, her goodwill. If she genuinely didn't feel like we could sell her name at some point down the road, we needed to change it soon so that we could become known under another umbrella. She thought about it and said, "I just can't imagine something bad happening and me standing in line at the grocery store and someone saying, 'That's Ms. Nancy,' when I no longer had anything to do with the program." That's how we did that. I and the assistant director and a staff member—I think we were sitting in the staff lounge one day, and the new name came to fruition out of our conversation.

Julie: It was just you all sitting around brainstorming.

Vernon: Isn't that the best way to get ideas, brainstorming?

Julie: Especially over lunch. It's funny, as we're going through these interviews, we hear these big strategic plans being laid out on a napkin over lunch.

Vernon: That's much better than the ones where you sit in the boardroom trying to stay awake.

Julie: Let's all put on our suits and ties and drink some coffee and try to come up with some strategic plans. It doesn't work. You have to unleash that creativity. That's a lot of thinking ahead on your and your mom's part to consider, "If we do want to sell some day, what's going to help the center be sellable?" That's what a lot of business owners don't think about: "Would I want to sell my business down the line? If I do, how would I approach that?" Even in my industry, speaking and consulting, coaches advise you to think about creating something you can resell later, if you want to sell your business.

Vernon: That's right. You have to think ahead. We all run thin margins, but you have to think ahead. Are you getting close to retirement? There are whole industries out there that will help child care programs prepare for the inevitability of it changing hands, of it going to either the next generation or going to an outside buyer. We all age, whether we want to or not.

Julie: That can be a whole different book topic.

Vernon: It's a stressful field. It's a hard-working, long-hours, stressful field. There does come a time when it's time to move on, and we have to be ready.

Julie: I know you're contemplating this, and there are other people in the industry thinking, *I know so much about staff development, the business side of this. Now I want to move on and share my expertise with others. Even if it's not about the stress or burnout or just the need to get out of it, it's growth for myself to be able to move myself to the next level.*

Vernon: Julie, that's why I went from one center to four. I was turning forty, and I really love the field I'm in. I have spent seventeen years, like I said, having taken down Bobby's paci and blanket and having the Biting 101 conversation. People kept telling me, when I was turning forty, "Okay, Vernon, it's all downhill from here." I thought to myself, *Downhill from here!? I haven't gotten to my pinnacle yet for me to start going downhill.* Instead of having an affair or buying a sports car convertible, I went out and bought three child care programs in eighteen months. I don't recommend that to anybody, because that is a lot of hard work. One of the hardest things I've ever done is try to get into a program that I've purchased that's been operational for years and try to change the culture. Changing the culture can be very difficult. I have been at that five or six years now. It's still a work in progress, but I think all programs are works in progress.

Julie: Absolutely. I think the key words that you said there were about culture and knowing what culture you want to bring. With a change in culture when you go and buy a center, it can be that you're going to lose staff, lose clients. You have to be really okay with who you are to let that happen.

Vernon: I had one program I purchased where there was genuine yelling going on in the program. I'd walk down the hallway, and they're yelling. You just can't do that. Ultimately we excused that staff member because that was her classroom management, to yell at the kids. We tried to coach her and give her other ways to deal with children, interact, get what she wanted out of the children. She just genuinely could not do it. Ultimately she chose to go somewhere else. I ran into a parent in town, and she said, "We sure are missing—" we'll say, "Ms. Sally." I said, "I'm so sorry. She was such a nice person, but don't you think the classroom management is better? There's a lot less yelling now." She looked around and said, "Well, Vernon, I guess there is, but I never considered it a problem, because I yell at my kids and I figured she could yell at my kids." That's the culture of that program. Not only was I having to change the staff members' outlook of what was appropriate in their interactions with children, but what I would consider inappropriate interaction with children, the parents thought was appropriate. In our world you think that if we fix that situation, parents would be happy, but that's not always the case.

Strategy 7
Control the message.

Julie: In this industry, one question we get asked a lot when parents are looking for quality child care in their area is, "How is turnover?" As a staff motivation expert myself, and I know you speak on the topic also, there's bad turnover and good turnover. There's turnover that we want to have happen. How do we get parents proactively to see that when turnover does happen, it's for the betterment of our child care program, for our child care business, for the culture that we want to cultivate?

Vernon: I think the first thing you have to do in that situation is the easiest thing—and people miss it—and that's inform the parent. Control the message. If you're depending on the assistant teacher who has worked with the teacher you just got rid of, or you realize a teacher was a D player and you just got rid of her or she walked out on you, and you're letting the assistant tell the parent what went down and how it went down and why, you are way behind the eight ball. Directors say, "I'm busy. I don't have time to send out a note." You must take time. You must take time to sit down and write a note. We all have cliques. We can ignore them, if we want to, in our programs. If you know there is a parent or two in charge of a clique, that they work together at a large employer— At one of my programs, we're down the street from a bank operation center. We get all that cubicle conversation, over the cubicles, about the kids in the program and who's potty trained and who's not, who can write and

59

who can't, and all this going on. If you know you have a ringleader at a company who brings lots of children to you, you need to call and tell that person what's going on. Of course, you don't talk derogatorily about staff, but you give the ringleader the big picture, so that when you hang up, the person understands your side of what went on.

Julie: This is so important. I think some of those steps we need to implement are so incredibly simple, like having proactive communication. It's all that negative mental mindset stuff that gets in the way, like, *The parents are going to leave. They're not going to like me. They'll think I did something wrong.* It's the time to jump out of that mindset and say, "Here are the steps to implement when this happens."

Vernon: I can assure you, ignoring it will not help.

Julie: No, it won't. Or even a general announcement, that doesn't help either.

Vernon: You have to be careful of that. That's something I train my directors on. If you have a staff member who leaves, let's say in your classroom of three-year-olds, I wouldn't send a note out to the entire program, to every child's parents. Directors often think they need to send a note out to everybody. That means a parent finds out about every staff member who's leaving. That's not necessary. You target which classroom the staff member works in. That's the group of children's parents you need to inform. You don't need to inform the entire program.

Julie: That's so true. You are incredibly connected with your desire in your heart to bring to fruition this vision you created with your child care program. What advice would you recommend to people to get connected with their vision and stay connected, so that when disaster strikes they don't lose their whole child care program, but instead could make four programs successful, like you have done? What advice would you give to them?

Strategy 8
Track your turnover rates.

Vernon: It's like the first thing I tell people if they're having turnover problems, that saying, "What gets measured gets done." I tell people to track their turnover so that they really, genuinely know what their turnover rate is. Again, people get busy, and they think they know. Then they start sitting down and considering, "Who was working in the three-year-old room before Sally was working there?"

Strategy 9
Have a vision.

That's how I feel about the vision. At some point you're sitting on the beach, or in your living room, drinking coffee. Get a pen and paper, or get on your iPad, laptop, doesn't matter. Start writing. Where do you see yourself going? Where do you see your program going? Put it down. Get it in writing. Have a vision. I believe that if you do something like that, it enacts parts of your brain that will work even behind the scenes, even when you sleep. It will work, and it will steer you in the right direction, to think positive and about where you're going and what you're going to do and what you want the outcome to look like. What's your end goal here? Where are you going to be? I think that's the first thing that someone needs to do. It's not a perfect thing. It's going to change. It has to be adapted over the years.

Julie: It's living and breathing. Alive.

Vernon: Absolutely, and it points you in the right direction.

Julie: I agree with what you're saying. Even by you doing that, sitting on a beach, writing things down, it really opens up your mind to the possibilities of what really is there for you.

Vernon: And it gets you out of thinking only about the mundane duties of day to day. Sometimes we have to step above it and do the big-picture work. Often we don't leave time to do the big-picture work because we're so engrossed in the little details that go on every day.

Julie: That's where we get stuck mentally. If you were to think about three factors that have really driven your business and helped you to become the successful business owner that you are, what would those three factors be?

Strategy 10

Staff members make or break you. Parents stay because of the relationships they have built with your staff.

Vernon: Wow! The first thing I would say is staff. Staff members make you or break you. You can have the best-run program, the best curriculum in the world. If you have really yucky staff, parents are not going to stay. We can fall into the false sense of, *Parents are here because of the components of my program, because we're teaching three-year-olds algebra and German*, or whatever it may be. Ultimately the parents stay because of the interaction and relationships built with your staff members.

Julie: I don't know whose biography I read many years ago, but it was a business owner's. He was standing there in his office looking out the window, watching his employees leave. One day he had an epiphany, *I'm watching the most important assets my company has leaving this program.* Without attachment to specific people, staff overall is the most important thing my business has.

Strategy 11

Staff members are customers.

Vernon: In child care specifically, the staff members are our customers, almost as much as our parents are our customers. We have to work at recruiting good staff, just like we have to work at recruiting parents into our program, and keeping them in our programs. I talk to people about protecting our good staff. We all have staff members who really are our shining stars. Those people, we need to make sure they know we think they're our shining stars. We need to make sure they genuinely feel appreciated. There's research after research that tells you people will fall under the false sense that everybody leaves for more money. That's just not true. People leave managers, not organizations. They leave their front-line managers because of not feeling appreciated, feeling the job they do is just expected, instead of feeling raised up as model individuals.

Julie: What I find too is that, when we're in a child care leadership role, we're paying attention to the people who are doing the wrong things. Those mistakes are just stabbing us like a knife demanding, *This has to change!* You feel you need to focus, focus, focus on correcting those problems. A shift in focus really brings that to light. It's almost an unnatural response to say, "Who are the people doing the right thing?"

Vernon: We spend so much time hiring and firing that we ignore the people in the middle doing the work. That has got to change in order to run a good organization. You have to balance it out. I think

I'll quote you for this. I think you told my directors at one of your retreats to hire slowly and fire quickly, or some phrase like that. That is so true. What you have to do is make sure you still spend time and build relationships with the people who are just there doing their job every day. We don't tend to pay any attention to them until they're about to leave. You have to be about it before something like that happens.

Julie: I don't know how this plays in, but it came to mind. We used to have a high school teacher who, every time somebody was doing anything wrong— Usually teachers will put those people closest to them. "You're going to sit right here with me." This one teacher I had, she would take everybody who was misbehaving, throwing notes, whatever, and she would move them to the backmost corner of the room. She did not want to give those people any of her attention. She did not want to help them learn if they weren't willing to help themselves. They were moved farthest away from her energy field. The ones who were doing the right things and studying, she would move those students up closer. It really stands out as a profound memory in my mind. Some people would say that's a bad teacher, but you're really putting your energy toward the ones who want to learn, without giving the distractions a second thought.

Vernon: She was ahead of her time.

Strategy 12

Work your budget.

Julie: Great staff would be one strength. What is another strength that has really contributed to your success?

Vernon: The other would be working your budget, putting it on paper. Again, another one of those things that people don't tend to do.

Julie: Look at your numbers.

Vernon: The money comes in, the money goes out. When the money is there, it goes out. When it's not there, they don't pay. They sit down and decide, *I'll pay Bobby this month, and I'll pay this and that next month.* It's just a paying game, basically. You've got to have a budget. The other thing is, you have to have a budget that works when you're not at 100 percent capacity. We all want to have our centers filled at 110 percent, but that's not reality all the time. In many programs, when their kids go on to kindergarten and enrollment drops down, they get in a panic or in a crisis situation. You've got to prepare. We know every year we're going to have a group of children go to kindergarten. It's not like it's a surprise. We know it's going to happen again next year, so let's have a plan.

That's what I would say. Make it work. Have money in reserves. Again, that's another phrase that the child care industry does not use a lot. Do they have reserves? If they have a crisis, if, heaven forbid, a natural disaster comes, can they sustain? Can they hold out for a month? What if there's a fire and they have to close, and it takes them a week or two weeks or two months to rebuild? What happens? Are their bills going to be able to be paid? Just having a budget and having it in writing, thinking through it and writing through it, is important. Not just in theory does a budget sound good, but it's important to have one that also works in practice.

Julie: I think that's the case for a lot of business owners, not just in the child care industry, but even just in general, with entrepreneurs. Look at your numbers, and get warm and fuzzy and have fun with those. So often, we look at them and then we want to run the other way, like you and your $135 paycheck.

Vernon: Absolutely.

Julie: Really embrace those numbers, look at them, and then have some fun with them.

Vernon: That's what makes it work.

Julie: We go through exercises, where we'll do cash flow analysis, where you look at thirty days. On the first day of the month, you have this much. Then you can plug in your bills and say, "Where do we need to change this so we're always meeting or exceeding these numbers?"

Vernon: Absolutely. Again, it goes back to "what gets measured gets done."

Julie: And what gets measured, we can improve upon.

Vernon: Absolutely. Then you genuinely have a goal, like turnover, enrollment or our budget. If we know where we were last year at this time, wouldn't it be great to look at, *Where are we going to be in December this year?* If we don't know that number or we can't get to it easily, it's just a moving target every year. Then we're being reactive instead of proactive.

Julie: Then it's really hard to put into place a growth strategy. Where do you want to go? Where is your growth going to happen? Do you have a third recommendation for us?

Vernon: I keep going back to staff. That's what I focus on so much. We talked about the business side and the staffing side.

Julie: We have staffing and numbers. I think mindset has got to be in there somewhere for you.

Vernon: I guess it would be visualizing the big picture, having the master plan of where we're going, what we're doing, where I'm going as an individual, what I'm doing, not only the organization but myself.

Julie: Mindset and vision just come into play in so many ways. It comes into play with relationships you build with parents. When you went through the natural disaster in 1999, you had the mindset to think, *We're going to go rent a building, and our parents are going to come and drive that hour to get to us.* That's a mindset. Some people would throw in the towel and say, "There's no way they're going to drive to this area where we're going to be chasing away homeless people."

Vernon: I knew that morning— I remember standing in the lobby of this center that we had rented, and in walk representatives from the health department. They said, "We heard you moved here, so we came to do an inspection." I remember at that point, that was my breaking point. I remember absolutely breaking down in tears with the health inspector, whom I had dealt with for ten years at that point. She realized, *Oh, this is too much, isn't it?* I remember thinking that if the kids did not show up, we wouldn't make it. But the kids showed up. I think sixty came the first day, and it grew from there. Keep in mind, my staff members were in a building with nothing but tables and chairs. There was not a toy, not a manipulative, not a matted play area, nothing. Parents, when they came in, they brought in bags of toys. Keep in mind, this is before Facebook. This is before any kind of social media. This is before we had parent e-mails. Our records were underwater. This was all word of mouth.

Julie: What do you do when you're in that moment, and you think, *Okay, we have to keep the parents*? Not only that, then you're going to grow to four centers. You're thinking, *I can't pay attention to the other child care programs that have the brighter and shinier and prettier objects. I just have to focus on my staff and who we are as people.* What kind of thoughts do you have when you're realizing, *Not only are we overcoming this natural disaster, but now we're going to grow* *into four different programs.* What goes through your mind when it comes to attracting dreamy clients and staff to come and be part of your vision? How do you go from that point of the disaster to four centers, not paying mind to the competition but growing and staying strong?

Vernon: People say you can't move forward when you're looking behind or side to side at your competitors. Partly that is true, but I will say I do some secret shopping, because I want to know what my competitors are telling people, how they're attracting people, what about their programs is attractive. What you have to do is just step back. Again, I couldn't do this when I was in the program working day to day to day on the small details. I couldn't see the big picture. Now I'm able to step back and observe the program from the outside in. What does it look like? Does it look warm? Does it look inviting? Does it look friendly? Does it look well maintained? Our brochure that goes home with prospective parents when they come for a tour, is it impressive? Does it stand up to the competition's? Is it copied on a crooked piece of paper, or folded, or could the director not find one? Those are all things that happen when you go into program centers. Staff get busy and hand parents a packet of information to complete, and the pages are twisted and crooked; they're making a copy of a copy. It just looks so disorganized.

Strategy 13
Keep calm and paddle like hell.

One strategy is that we usually try to look extremely organized. It reminds me of the picture that floated around decades ago of the little duck where, above water, he looked so calm, and underneath he was paddling like hell. That's kind of what you have to do in this business, and many businesses. To your parents, it's just a calm, serene day here at Wee School. Underneath, we are working like dogs to try to keep up with our own expectations. I think that's one thing we have to do. You need to have expectations for your program. I always tell my staff, "When I stop pushing you, you know there's something wrong." When I stop having a vision of the next step, when there is no next step, I will know it's time for me to go. There's always a next step. There's always a place for growth and professional development.

Strategy 14
Remember, it's always your choice.

That's one thing I've talked to directors about. We've chosen this field. People can say, "I'm in early childhood, but I'm thinking I might do something else," or "This is just a meantime job until something better comes along." I'll respond, "Honey, if you've been making donuts for ten years, you're a donut maker. Embrace it and move on. When was the last time you read a book on leadership, a book on staffing, a book on early childhood, a book on discipline, a book on curriculum?" They'll just look at me, and I'll add, "It's your career. Treat it like it is." You have to take time. I'm not saying you have to live it and breathe it 24/7, but we're all part of growing and nurturing. Our programs become better, and that's part of it.

Julie: I had the opportunity to talk with other staff management experts, and they recommend one of the top techniques for avoiding burnout and reducing the stress you're feeling is to not be victimized by a choice you made. If you're in this industry thinking, *Oh, my gosh!*, you have to realize, *Why am I here?*

Vernon: Absolutely right. That also goes into taking that excuse away from our staff members. We have been programmed, and we have programmed our staff over the years, to think, *Woe is you. You're overworked and underpaid.*

69

Julie: Let me get you donuts.

Vernon: Right. It is what it is. Our pay is what it is. If our pay could be more, we would pay more. I know thousands of early childhood business owners. They are good-hearted people. If they had more money in their budgets, they would share it with their staffs. They're paying what they can afford. It doesn't help. It doesn't move us forward to just continue to sit back and say, "Woe is our staff. They make no money. They work so hard." That's just a given. We have to move on with that.

Julie: I agree. That's one of the biggest transformations I see with clients I work with, that transformation in mindset from *we're victimized by this* to *we're empowered by this*.

Strategy 15
Remember your why.

When we talk about why you do what you do and why you chose this, the question I have for you is, Why is it this industry for you? What does it mean to you?

Vernon: Julie, that gives me one of those misty kinds of moments. This sounds so cheesy, but I just love to see kids' expressions when they are in their classrooms and engaged, and the staff member is engaged, and that classroom is running effortlessly. They're playing water play, painting at the easel, doing Play-Doh. They're doing all the things that people whose hearts and souls are not into it will tell you can't be done. It can be done. That is why I'm there. That's my moment of fulfillment, when I can walk out of a classroom with a smile and think, *That teacher rocks*. I also make sure I turn around and say, "You rock!"

Strategy 16
Take time for yourself.

Julie: That's very powerful. When it comes to being successful in this industry, we talked earlier a little bit about really being able to define your own self-worth as a business owner. I know you've progressed tremendously on this journey in sharing with us why you do what you do, the disaster you've overcome, and now having four successful centers. What do you do at this point? How do you feel about your self-worth and your self-care? Are there routines that you go through to make sure that you, Vernon, are taken care of as you become a more powerful leader in this industry?

Vernon: I make sure I take time for myself. I read professional development books. I also read things for pleasure. I take time. I will tell you that I put in a lot of hours. It's kind of like what I tell parents when they come into my program for a tour. If I happen to do the tour, I'll say, "When we play, we play hard. When we work, we work hard." That's how I am as a person. When I am working, I'm all about working. When I play, I'm all about play. I try to make sure I take significant time off during the year. I try my best to take time off where I can completely disconnect. I try to have people in place that will handle everything but extreme emergencies. They know they can call me in the event we have a genuine emergency that I need to handle or give input on.

I try to surround myself with people who help support my vision. That goes for anything from your insurance agent to— I have what we call a fractional human resources person who works for me a few hours a week. We can't afford an HR department, but we have someone who works for us four hours a week who handles our HR issues. She's available 24/7. I can call her anytime to run things by her, how to handle situations, things like that. The same with our payroll company. I just work on surrounding myself with people who are there to support our program, because I cannot do it all. When I realized that you can pass some of the big responsibility on to other people, it became a much lighter burden to carry.

Julie: Very good.

Strategy 17

Be genuine.

I ask child care owners what they want to know from other child care owners, and this is probably the same question parents want to ask. "What makes you different? When it comes to your child care program, what makes you different?"

Vernon: Believe it or not, Julie, I struggle with that some. That's something that is on my big-range vision, to sit down and think about that, to have a day with my directors to have some sharing and figure out what exactly those differences are. I think we're a program that strives to do what's best for children on a daily basis, and not teach to the test but fulfill our expectations on a daily basis. When parents see us do that on a daily basis and don't see things change, even if we're coming up for a big inspection or something like that, they realize we're genuine. That, I think, is a difference compared to some other outcomes.

I also believe that there has been a lot revealed in the last decade or two about play and how children learn to play. I do believe that. I also know that there is a rigorous world out there, and that when kids get to kindergarten, they need to be able to write their names. They need to be able to recognize most of the alphabet. I think sending children to school not knowing things like that puts them behind. Sometimes it hurts our industry, I think, because the "best" programs sometimes will have that environment where it's just an all-play environment. When kids get to school— I'm not saying they don't catch up, and I'm not saying the kids aren't bright or get where they need to, but initially they're behind the eight ball. I think sometimes that turns people off to our field. It hurts our reputation, and people think, *They don't do anything but play. They don't really learn.* We do stress **fun learning** in our program.

Julie: I think you've touched upon something that's critically important. I encourage all of our listeners to write this down. One of the things I just got from you is that part of the way you're different is by being authentic and genuine. Not to say that other people aren't genuine, but imagine, if everybody were authentic and genuine, wouldn't we naturally be different?

Strategy 18
You're in the sales business.

Vernon: When I've had my secret shoppers go out to other programs, some of the things that other programs do is really talk about what their competitors do wrong instead of talking about what they're doing right. When you go in for a tour in certain programs, they're tearing other people down. That's their marketing style, I guess, and maybe it works for some people. Believe in your program. Believe in your strengths. It is about the heart. It is about relationships. We are in the sales industry. We are selling a product, and that product is our child care program.

Julie: If you are a business, what drives the business to success? It's always sales. That's an excellent point. One last question for you, Vernon. Who's been an inspiration to you?

Vernon: Who's been an inspiration to me? Well, I have to begin with my mother. My mother taught me by my watching her interact with the children she cared for in our home, and treating those children respectfully and kindly, and making sure those kids knew—She had peers she knew who cared for children. They'd say, "Nancy, why are you teaching them the alphabet? They don't need to know that. They can learn that when they get to school." My mother was determined. This was in the late '80s and early '90s. My mother, even then, wanted to make sure the kids were prepared for school.

Holly Elissa Bruno is an inspiration to me on the management style of dealing with staff members. Paula Jorde Bloom is an inspiration. She was the head of our master's degree program. I call her the Energizer Bunny. She just taught me such great things about meetings, staff meetings, coaching people and things like that. And Becky Bailey with her conscious discipline has been such an inspiration. I cannot forget Rushmi Nakri. You've probably never heard that name. She was a local individual here in my town. I met her, and she became my peer. She ran a very large nonprofit program in town. She is now retired. We discovered how much in common she and I had. We would go to lunch and laugh because she was nonprofit and I was for-profit, but her salary was higher than mine. It just broke down the barrier of "the for-profits make all the money and they're greedy" and "the nonprofits are all about the children." Neither one of those analogies is correct. It was just very enlightening to both of us and how much we have in common.

Julie: That's a great list of inspirations. Is there anything that you would like to say in closing, anything I haven't asked you that you really want to get out there?

Vernon: You've done such a good job. I can't really think of anything.

Julie: When we first started this series, I told people, "I've interviewed Jack Canfield, Zig Ziglar, Les Brown, all the motivational superstars. Now it's my absolute pleasure to interview the superstars in the child care industry." I'm delighted that you're one of them.

Vernon: I'm honored that you would ask me, Julie. It's an honor to be interviewed by you.

Update: Vernon Mason, Jr., is the author of Don't Go: A Practical Guide For Tackling Employee Turnover *which is available on Amazon.com. Through his book and speaking engagements, he continues to inspire child care owners and directors beyond the four centers he owns and operates. He recently spoke at Julie's Child Care Business Success Conference and left people breathless from laughing so hard at his tell-all tales of the life he's led as a hands-on owner and director.*

To hear this interview in its entirety, go to **www.ChildCareBusinessSuccess BookVault.com**. The password is **RockMyChildCare.com**.

Chapter 4

The Ultimate Game Changer

Featuring Brandi Gibson,
Brandi's Place

"If you are working on something exciting that you really care about, you don't have to be pushed. The vision pulls you."

Steve Jobs

Having a strong, compelling vision in place was the game changer for Brandi Gibson and Deb Cramer, co-owners and co-directors of Brandi's Place. These two ladies simply shine, as their individual personalities set them apart from any other child care program in Swartz Creek, Michigan. Their award-winning child care program was brought to life in 2004. Just like many other child care programs, theirs is a family affair.

Opening a month late didn't faze this dynamic mother-daughter duo as they accommodated the handful of children at Brandi's own home until they opened the doors of their new building. Brandi, a former nanny with a degree in family studies, personally cared for the children until their 9,000-square-foot building, constructed from the ground up by Deb's father (Brandi's grandfather), Del Pratt, was ready to open.

When the business moved into the new building, only one of the nine classrooms was full. Brandi found that more than a little scary. Enrollments needed to be filled and filled fast to help them become a thriving child care business. Today, the center has more than 130 children and a cohesive staff consisting of more than twenty teachers and assistants.

Brandi credits the cohesiveness to the unbeatable combination of the business developing a vision statement that everyone understands and respects, and having a business coach only a phone call away. These days, decisions are made in line with the vision. Staff members know each other's responsibilities and easily can step in for each other as needed, and all of the processes are in order, including having all of the necessary forms easily accessible.

Read on to learn how having a businesswide vision has been such a game changer for Brandi that, for the first time ever—after nearly ten years on the job—she felt comfortable leaving the business for a full week so she and her husband could take a much-deserved vacation!

Strategy 1

Good, old-fashioned PR builds recognition and trust.

Julie: Less than nine years after opening your doors, you worked yourself up to the place where you're one of the Best of the Best for 2013. That was a nice award to get. Tell us a little bit about that. That's where the community votes for you, right?

Brandi: The community has, in the local newspaper, a form you can fill out for all different types of business in the area. You fill out what you believe is the best in that area. We just happened to win the Best of the Best for our area, just by people in the community voting.

Julie: What do you think did it for you, getting that award?

Brandi: Being out in the community. We volunteer a lot, help out at the schools a lot, just working with children, working with our chamber of commerce, just being out there and interacting.

Julie: That's really important. I think that's a huge trust builder too, when you're out there doing charity work, being involved in the community and in different groups. I think that's really important. Are there any groups that you have found to be critical to the success that you've created over the past years?

Brandi: I think working with the schools has a huge influence. We work closely with the teachers. They're very helpful. They can tell you, "Our standards are changing, so the kids coming into kindergarten are going to need to know this." It's nice to know so that we can make sure our kids here are ready for kindergarten. Then the word gets out, so word of mouth is important too.

Julie: That's what I was going to ask you. When you first opened your doors nine years ago, was it a little scary thinking, *Where are our clients going to come from?*

Brandi: We were supposed to open in June. We got set back a month. We had only a very small number of kids registered at the time in this huge building. I had these kids at my own home until we could open. When we started, I think there were eight kids. It was very scary because we didn't know— We have these bills to pay, and where are we going to go? It's led us up to where we are now, a situation when we have no worries.

Julie: So from eight kids, it was a leap to being fine?

Brandi: It was a struggle. We've had our moments. I would say the first year was really rough, and then it got a little better. Probably about the third or fourth year, it was really tough. The economy dropped and people were losing their jobs. We struggled. We were still doing okay, but every day it felt like, *Oh, my gosh, tuition came in and now it's all gone.*

Julie: So there have definitely been some growing pains. That's good for you, our readers, to hear, because you're not alone. If you're having challenges, if you're trying to create a business, you're going to have challenges.

Brandi: And you can't give up. A lot of people give up, and we were not going to do that. It will work.

Julie: How quickly did you go from eight kids to sixteen to twenty-four?

Brandi: The first year we grew quite a bit. Then we kind of stayed where we were at. We would lose kids and gain kids. We were never getting ahead. We lost two, gained two, lost one, gained two. Then we were one up, and then a family of three left. It felt like we were piggybacking for so long. Then a lot of the marketing that we've done, even just the past two years, has really made a huge difference in our staff. We've had staff who have left, and then come back, and even said, "I don't want to be anywhere else. This is where I want to be." Generally we don't rehire, but we have in the past.

Julie: Experts, including me, say that the grass always looks greener on the other side.

Brandi: Exactly.

Julie: Once you get to the other side, the greener pastures are behind you. That's a big strategy in itself. I always recommend to people, "Don't close those doors on rehiring old staff, because some of them may come back and be really amazing for you. Keep those doors open." So, you have found a couple of good people who've come back to you.

Strategy 2

Be present.

I think you're doing more than one thing right. We asked people on our Facebook page, "What is it that you would like to know as we interview all these successful child care business owners?" They said the one thing they would really like to know is, What makes you different? I think they're trying to figure out their uniqueness and how they're different, how they should go and sell themselves to the parents in the community. When you think about how you're different, what is it that you've done or implemented or believe that everybody on your staff should do to make you different?

Brandi: Ours is family-oriented. We're not a franchise center. I really don't want to become that. Our families are treated as our own families. We love each and every one of them. They know there are boundaries. They try to push them sometimes. That's one way that we like to say we stand out from others. There's always a director onsite. Some centers don't have a director from open to close. There are three of us here. There is always someone who opens and always someone who closes. In almost ten years, we've left only once, and that was to see you. It was a good choice. There's always someone here. I think that makes a big difference when there's always someone to answer the phone, always someone at the front door. That way the teachers can put their energy into their classrooms and their kids, and they're not having to worry about watching the front desk, answering the phones. That's just something that we do here.

Julie: How many kids and staff do you have right now?

Brandi: We have twenty-three teachers and one hundred eleven kids.

Julie: Your leadership team consists of you, the co-owner, Deb Cramer, who is your mother, and then you have wonderful Mandy Hense in place. It's the three of you who alternate leadership. Mandy is your office person and assistant director, right?

Brandi: Yes.

Julie: So she helps manage staff and do all the office work. That's good. You feel that someone being onsite makes you different. What else makes you different? I know you guys have done some crazy intensive work, especially this past year, in terms of establishing your difference more. We want to hear some of these juicy details. I think the growth that you've been through will help everybody else to realize, *Oh, I can go through that too, and I'll be okay.* I'm hoping what this series does for everybody who's reading is that they're learning these nuggets of gold from everybody. Because it takes you four years, five years, nine years, twenty years on this journey, but their success can be expedited. They're hearing and learning from these people like you who have been there and done that.

Brandi: For sure.

Julie: Tell us a little bit more about your journey.

Strategy 3

Have a strong, compelling vision.

Brandi: Having a vision. We never had that before. That was a huge thing, to have a vision, making sure our staff is on the same page. At every staff meeting, that's something we pull out. We actually made up a poster board and had it professionally done. At the meeting, that's one of the first things we go over. I think that makes a difference for us that you can go back and say, "Is that in line with our vision statement for our staff?" We didn't have that before.

Julie: Before, was it just that you didn't think of having one?

Brandi: We just didn't know. I don't want to say we were flying by the seat of our pants, but we kind of were.

Julie: That's what a lot of my clients say. They didn't realize the vision is really that piece. A lot of times we think, *Why won't our staff get off their cell phones? Why won't they do this? Why won't they do that? We really don't have the strong, compelling vision that we're leading our team with.* Establishing that vision, I think, was really critical for you this year.

Strategy 4
Let your vision guide you.

Brandi: Yes, very. It made a huge, huge difference. It's more looking at the positives and not dwelling on the negatives. That was huge. The gossiping and the drama, it's hard because you're hearing different stories from six people and trying not to get caught in the middle of it, taking sides. It doesn't have to do with our vision statement. We're not having this negativity. Getting rid of all that and letting our staff know that we're not tolerating that anymore.

Julie: That's big. In this industry, even though we logically can grasp the idea that there shouldn't be gossip and this and that, a lot of times our focus goes from *Do we pay attention to the vision?* to *Do we pay attention to the staff, because we need happy staff members in place?* We really get torn between the focus of our priorities until we get crystal clear on it: If we don't have a vision, everything that we're doing is going to fall apart. We've got to stay dedicated to that. I remember that being part of your big growth too, not only realizing you need a vision, but also all the different pieces that vision impacts.

Brandi: It's not just the staff. It's the parents, the community, all of that.

Julie: It's everything. I always remember the saying, "Where there's no vision, the people will perish." It means all people—not just the people under you, but the people around you. Your vision is your guiding light for what you're doing. Can you give us a little bit of before you established that vision and after—what the day was like before and then what the day was like after you had that strong, compelling vision in place?

Brandi: Oh, goodness, do you really want to know what the day before was like?

Julie: You can give us a little hint. I'm sure people can relate. Just judging from that, we know it wasn't good.

Brandi: It was coming into work: What kind of fires do we have to put out today? What's the latest gossip going on today? What kinds of problems are we going to have today? Even myself, not wanting to come in, the anxiety of *I don't want to deal with it. I have my own home and kids to take care of.* I want to be able to come into work and do my work and have fun and go home. The gossiping, the cell phones, the lack of respect, an unmotivated team, that's what we were before.

Strategy 5
Good boundaries make all the difference.

Julie: You also have a dynamic because the co-owner is your mom. It was also just working through these relationships. This is very common in this industry, where we have either a husband and wife, mom and daughter, or two sisters working together and running the business. There are personal issues that just can't help but come up. You have that dynamic as well.

Brandi: Now it's wonderful. In the office, we have a responsibility chart. It has all our names—mine, Mandy's, Debbie's. It has a list of all the things we do. It has a section that says "All Directors." That's stuff we can all work on together, things like keeping staff on track or assisting staff with supplies, or doing tours, tasks that all three of us can do. That way, nobody is stepping on anyone's toes. Nobody is doing work twice. I didn't do it and then somebody turns around and does it behind me, or I didn't do something somebody else already did. It's nice knowing that our roles are defined now.

Julie: I think it eliminates the power struggles too. It often happens just between co-workers. If you have two teachers in a classroom, there can be a power struggle that happens.

Brandi: The responsibility chart made a huge, huge difference for us. Looking back, our situation before the chart was, *I think I'm helping her*, but I really wasn't. It was creating anxiety and, *She did my job again*. Or, *It wasn't done correctly*. Now it's, "Do you need help with that?" If we see someone needs help, then we help each other. If not, that's your job and you do it. If one of us is gone, we just pitch in and each does the other person's job. It's really helped us. Regarding the staff, the responsibility chart has helped us with the gossiping and knowing that we're not tolerating it anymore, and getting it through to them that we're not tolerating it. For the cell phones, we have invested in lockers for the girls. Now they have their own lockers with their own combination locks. They have no reason to take anything into the classrooms with them. That's something that before we would never have been able to invest in. It was kind of nice that we were able to put the money out for those. They can put their purses and cell phones in there. They just know we're not tolerating it. If you're caught, you are written up. We have caught them, but we don't have a problem going in and asking them, "Do you have your cell phone on you?" Before, we would have never done that. It would be, *Oh, my gosh, we're going to make them mad*. We don't care anymore.

Julie: Part of being a successful business owner in any industry is really being, again, committed to that vision and not caring so much what people think, to a level. We have to have happy employees, but it's not caring about what they think so they'll like us. There's a difference between caring because we want them to like us and caring because we want our vision to come to fruition.

Brandi: A big thing for us—it really hit home, and I'm sure it did for my mom—it's their choice. It's not our choice if they get fired. It's their choice. And making them see they can't blame us. You chose that direction of not changing what needed to be changed. It was your choice to leave. We have had to put that back on people. We actually had an employee where we said, "Here it is in writing. You can take it home. You can think about it. If you're going to choose to stay, here are the changes that need to be made. If you choose to leave, you need to sign this and resign." She left, but that was her choice. We would have never done that before.

Julie: I love that. We have to really help people understand that if an employee leaves, it is that employee's choice, and to be able to frame it in that way too. There is specific dialogue you can use. If I'm doing my job right, they should know they're choosing whether they stay here or not. I think the fault part comes into play when we're not, as leaders, doing our jobs correctly. Then we just get so frustrated with what's going on that we want to go and fire everybody. As long as we're doing our job right, they should be able to make the choice of whether they're going to be fired or if they're going to stay. That's powerful.

Brandi: The only other boundaries issue I can really think of that stands out is the friendship. There's a fine line between friendship and business, and teaching our staff where that line is. Outside of here is a different story, but when we're at work, it's business. You can't put your personal emotions into your job. We're not always going to be liked. We're not always going to be your friend. Sometimes we have to be the bad guy, but you can't get mad at us for it.

Julie: After this whole growth process, how different do you, your mom and Mandy now feel about your jobs and your day?

Brandi: It's night and day. It really is. Before it was just always feeling like, *This has to be done, this has to be done, that has to be done.*

I've got to get in there and get this done. We've been open for nine and a half years. Usually I take vacations, a Friday, Monday and Tuesday. This is the first year my husband and I actually went on a cruise Monday through Friday. I went the whole week with no communication with the child care, and I was fine.

Julie: I saw pictures, and it looked like you were having a blast.

Brandi: It was a good relief. I called when we got back to the airport on Saturday. I called my mom and let her know we were back on American soil and we'd be home in a little bit. It was just talking about our kids, how the kids did. It wasn't about work. It's nice to know that I can go home and spend time with my kids and my family and I don't have to worry about that. Whoever is here, any of us directors, that person can take care of it. It's a relief knowing we don't all have to be here, all at the same time, all the time.

Julie: What a transformation. A lot of people struggle with that. They do go home. They do talk about business. They can't stop thinking about business. They're up at two o'clock in the morning writing down notes and things that are on their minds that they're still worried about the next day.

Brandi: That has happened. I know it's happened to all three of us. My mom said it's happened to her. Mandy has said it happened to her. It happened to me. I haven't had that—knock on wood—in a long time, which is a blessing.

Strategy 6
Get a coach.

Julie: That's so good. You stepped out this year. We met about a year and a half ago, something like that. One of the things that really sets

Brandi's Place apart is just being willing to invest in themselves, to say, "We need help. We can't do this alone." You guys sought me out and said, "Okay, let's coach. Let's work together." Maybe you can tell us a little bit more about this, because I think coaching can still be new to people in this industry who never worked with a coach for their business before. A lot of times we bring in coaches to help us with curriculum or with the academic side of things, the state licensing, whatever it might be. Let's talk a little bit about your journey in working with a coach, myself, over the past year. It is such a viable option for everybody to really get involved, get support. You don't have to go it alone.

Brandi: For us it's been amazing. We met you at a conference. Just listening to you speak, I believe it was when you were having the first ten or twenty people up there. I was number one. I was like, *I've got to meet this lady. I've got to know her. I need her help.* I still have the flash drive that was given to me that day. Just looking at the stuff and going to the website, having access to the website and the forms that are on there. It's stuff you don't think about, like a substitution form. I never thought about that. We have our black book in the classroom where, if a teacher is sick and a substitute has to go in there or a different teacher has to go in there, they can open up the book and see all the activities for the day. If you know you're going to have a day off, why not have that form and make it easier for the person taking over for you?

Julie: That also brings up another great point, about getting your processes in line. Forms are part of the processes you have in place. You can print out all these forms. For our high-level clients, we have a whole membership community where you can log in and get all these forms Brandi is talking about, and access some really cool resources. Your time is so valuable. You have to think about, *Am I doing $5-an-hour work or $10-an-hour work? Am I really focusing on the $100-an-hour work or the $1,000-an-hour work?* That's more of your marketing and public relations, as opposed to things you would do repetitively.

Brandi: There are so many forms out there that you don't think about. It was wonderful to go in, and it's like, *Oh, yeah, I didn't think about that one. Oh, I need this one. I need this one too.* It's the little things, like the substitution form or the complaint form. Is there a problem? Have someone fill out the information. That way, it's confidential. Someone doesn't have to worry about, *Oh, she was in the office. What were they talking about?* They can just fill out a form, drop it in the back, and we can take care of it without anyone knowing who it was from. The newsletters and all of that has made a huge difference. Then attending your three-day intensive was like night and day for us. I love being around you anyway, all that positive energy. It really makes a person feel good. That was a life-changing thing. You could take the stuff we learned there and even use it at home. Sometimes I have to catch myself. I'm like, *No, no, that's not what I learned. I need to back up and do this the right way.* Our staff meetings used to be boring.

Julie: Even *you* would make up excuses not to come.

Brandi: Right. It was like, *I don't want to go. It's going to be all negative. I don't want to hear all that stuff.* Now, the way we do our staff meetings is we each have a half-hour. I get a half-hour, my mom gets a half-hour, and Mandy gets a half-hour. You have to pick an activity and do something that's a team-building or an interactive-type activity. When I do mine, I also talk about the things that need to be changed, or the things that are happening that we need to really address, and why we're having the meeting. We still get to do the interactive things. The staff really like coming now versus before.

Julie: That's fantastic. So a lot fewer excuses. We hear that a lot too. A lot of organizations struggle, *Oh, my goodness, they have school,* *this birthday*, whatever it is. You can facilitate those staff meetings so that people can't wait for the next one.

Brandi: How we're doing it is, even if we don't have anything to discuss, we're still going to have a meeting. Every other month we have a group meeting, and every other month we do individual meetings. With the individual meetings, you're assigned a time to come in. You have ten minutes to spill your guts, what needs to be fixed, what you need from us, how we can support you, what we need to make sure you have the tools to do your job correctly. The teachers like that too, because sometimes it's hard to think of things. If they don't have anything, on the questionnaire, it says, "If you don't have anything to discuss, here's a question that you can come planned to answer." That way we're not just sitting in here staring at each other.

Julie: So working with a coach, how instrumental was that to your growth?

Brandi: Huge. We would have never done any of that stuff before.

Julie: This is something that I really preach to people to be aware of, that desire you feel. The desire might be, *Oh, my goodness, I need to be around that person. I need to work with that person.* I believe that's the universe trying to give you a message as to the direction you need to go in order to get you to the next level of success. You listened.

Brandi: I did. I'm glad I did.

Julie: I'm glad you did too. It's been a real pleasure working with you. What is your vision going forward? What do you want to bring to fruition?

Brandi: Continue on the road we're going, having a good, motivated staff, being recognized in the community as the leader of child care services, just always being known and being out there, even just being helpful. I had a parent come in today whose family is becoming a foster family. He said, "I don't even know if I'm going to need day care, but I need to make sure I'm prepared." I had the forms ready for him, and I can sympathize with him. We've been there. We've had families like that before. Even when he left, he said, "I can't thank you enough. Nobody else was wanting to help me like that. It was, 'Here's your tour. Have a good day.'" So just being able to communicate with people out in the community and help them, I want to keep going in that direction and do better.

Strategy 7
Find your winning formula.

Julie: Yes, keep building upon that. What's the biggest thing you've done to grow your enrollment? Do you think it's all the same as what you've done to grow your staff, that it's about growing yourself? Or do you think there's a magical technique that people can implement?

Brandi: I think it's a combination of all. I think you need to have good staff. That's who's going to go out and say, "I like my job. Bring your kids here. I'll take good care of them." We have a great team. I think that's a huge thing, being known in the community. I had an appointment last week and she said, "Oh, you must be Brandi from Brandi's Place over on Hill Road." I didn't know this lady. She knew who I was, but I didn't know her.

Julie: Getting some of that celebrity status.

Brandi: Being out there and having the good staff, being known, having good parents. Your parents are, to me, a big marketing thing. They're going to go out there and say, "I take my kids here, and you need to go here." Being involved in the schools and having teachers say, "I've had kids from this center, and this center, and this center. The kids that come from Brandi's Place are ready for kindergarten." I think that's a huge thing too.

Julie: If you were to look at your program in terms of the different components, you have attracting parents, parents who come in for tours, then parents who convert and your open houses. Is there anything that you feel you do that's really special in terms of how you treat your parents? We've heard a little of how you're treating your staff these days. Is there anything that you feel you do that is just your special touch that's authentically you because of who you are?

Brandi: I just think having a director there all the time and just always being there, able to answer questions. Even though you can't make everyone happy, just be sympathetic with them. They're part of our family. Without our parents, we're not here. They're the ones who are paying for everything. So trying to make them happy, within reason—they have to follow the rules too—but have that respect for them. You see it a lot in different stores. People just come to work for a paycheck. I think for us, being sympathetic and always acknowledging them. There's never someone who walks through this door who we don't say "Good morning" to, or "Have a good day," or "Be careful driving." We acknowledge everyone.

Julie: One of your recent accomplishments that you're pretty excited about is your website, BrandisPlace.com. I love the little puppet guy who greets you when you first come in, who shows you the importance of Brandi's Place in your greeting. Even on your website you have Mr. Puppet saying hello to you.

Brandi: We just call him Habeeb. We don't have a name for him.

Julie: Tell us a little about your website and what kind of impact that has had on your business.

Brandi: We had that built last summer, I believe. We've gone through a lot to get it to where it's at now. That has been a huge marketing piece for us as well, having people go there. It basically has everything on there, anything from activities that are going on, to pictures that we've had, to how we started. If the center is closed—which we very rarely close, but there was a day that we had all that snow and we did close—we can put that up on the website.

Julie: This is something that everyone should really have on their website—what you have on BrandisPlace.com—the free report. Brandi's is "How To Choose An Amazing Childcare Center." Has that one been downloaded a lot?

Brandi: We get e-mails letting us know when it's been used. It gets used more often than I thought it was going to.

Julie: The cool thing about having that—what we call an "irresistible offer"—on your front page is that you're able to capture those leads from parents who think, *Oh, yes, I want to know how to choose an amazing child care center.*

Brandi: The other process we're starting to add, when we do tours, we have a bag that they get. We've never done this before. The bag has a folder with our handbook and all the forms they need. It's got little goodies in there. Right now we have notepads, a pen and hand sanitizer. We've given out coffee mugs before. We've given out children's books. There's always something in there that's a goodie they get to take away with them. It's a marketing piece as well. In there it has all the handbooks. In the handbook packet, we've now created a "What to Look for in a Childcare Center" as well. It's one page. If they don't go to our website, they still have it in front of them. We want people to know these are the things to look for. People don't understand some of the qualities to look for in a good child care center. I think that's the big information to get out.

Julie: That's another thing one of our guests said, I think Bill Grant from Hildebrandt Learning Centers. He really sees it as educating the community on how to pick child care and who they are. It's really important to look at it from that perspective. Your website is bright and colorful. I encourage everybody to go there. I think most of the important components are there. You've got your "About Us" page. I love that, because you can see them breaking ground nine years ago with your sign and your building. When you originally established, did you get some publicity around that?

Brandi: There was an article in the paper. When we first opened, we did another article in the paper as well, about the mother-daughter team that's built this beautiful building. I talked about my kids. At the time I had only one, my son. It was kind of nice that I got to take him in to work. It talked about that, a little bit of the personal, and then how we got to where we were and built that, and where we planned to go.

Julie: A lot of great stuff there. Brandi, is there anything you'd like to say in closing?

Brandi: Make sure you have your vision. I'm never going to live that down. I'm not going to let it go.

Julie: That's a big piece of what we're teaching. We realized after doing this for seventeen years and working with our business owners that it was missing. Not a lot of people are teaching it and talking about it to this industry. It's crucial.

Brandi: And have a coach that you can go to. It's nice to know that if we have a problem or I have a question, I can shoot you an e-mail or give you a call, "I need help. I don't know what to do." Don't let your anxiety build up and up and up to where you're going to explode. You have somebody you can go to who can help you and walk you through that.

Julie: You don't have to do it alone. Sometimes on our phone calls, how long does it take for that pressure to be relieved from you?

Brandi: Not very long.

Julie: Sometimes I know you suffer with issues, and I'm not just talking about Brandi. You can struggle with things for what might seem like weeks. Then you can pick up the phone, call your coach and talk with her for five minutes.

Brandi: "Now I feel so much better. Now let me go do what she's telling me to do." It's all taken care of.

Julie: Get a coach. See who pulls at your heart. See what the desire is. I always say that's how I've been attracted to my coaches in my life. It's just, *Who do I feel magnetized toward? Who's pulling at me?* Also, with your vision, know that it's not just a one-time document. It is a living, breathing thing that can change and grow as you do, as I'm sure you're experiencing a little bit.

Update: Brandi's Place continues to be voted The Best of The Best 2014, 2015 and 2016!

To hear this interview in its entirety, go to **www.ChildCareBusinessSuccess BookVault.com**. The password is **RockMyChildCare.com**.

Chapter 5

Higher Profits Is the End Result

Featuring Jane Porterfield and Gerry Pastor, Educational Playcare

"If you want to see the sunshine, you have to weather the storm."

Frank Lane

*E*very year for the past four years, their company has grown by 20 percent, and in 2014 it was recognized by Child Care Information Exchange as one of North America's largest for-profit child care programs. Their core belief is to continuously provide high value to the families they serve while investing in their own growth, as business owners, and the growth of their staff. Because of how they serve their community, they are getting media recognition and more! Who are they? Meet Jane Porterfield and Gerry Pastor.

I first met Jane and Gerry while I was speaking about managing, motivating and retaining great staff at an event. Without much hesitation they signed on with me to come to their programs and help them with what they felt was "the missing link" for them at that time—staff motivation. This is only one reason why I truly adore this husband and wife team, who are the owners of Educational Playcare in Connecticut. Today their business has seven locations (Simsbury, Farmington, Wallingford, West Hartford, Windsor, Avon and East Hampton) and is licensed for 1,590 children. Two additional locations are scheduled to open during the coming year.

This is where they are now, but Gerry states that they had to weather the perfect storm, time and time again, to get to this place with their child care business success. After seeing a "perfect storm" bankrupt him in his previous career, Gerry says when he started working with Jane right after she had opened her second center, they borrowed money everywhere they could to survive. "Both of our parents helped us, and it was amazing how much we could borrow on our credit cards at the time," he says.

Here's how their journey began.

It was 1986, and Jane Porterfield, fresh out of graduate school, had the idea to start a child care business that included a comprehensive educational program, so that children wouldn't have to be taken elsewhere for nursery school. She came up with the name Educational Playcare while throwing around various names with her parents. There was no real magic to it except knowing that the educational component was very important to her.

Jane opened her first location in Avon, Connecticut, with a couple of children and one other staff member. In 1995, she opened her second building, with eighty children all starting the day it opened. (In retrospect, she says that wasn't a good idea!)

As she raised their four children at a time when Gerry traveled a lot, Jane knew how busy parents are with their day-to-day lives, and she wanted not only to offer quality child care but also to facilitate the entire experience for their families. She started having someone come to the center once a month to offer haircuts, and began transporting children to dance and gymnastics classes as well as other extracurricular activities during the day.

With the bankruptcy of the insurance company Gerry had been running (due to factors that preceded his assuming control), he was looking for a new position. But, an actuary by background, he was overqualified for positions in the Hartford area. Rather than relocate the family, he decided to weather this storm with grace and move into the child care world with Jane. He started out by taking care of maintenance. He painted, fixed toilets, mopped and waxed floors . . . whatever it took to help out. Today he and Jane are joined at the hip in their management of a company that has grown to more than two hundred fifty employees.

This dynamic duo has come a long way in creating a successful child care business!

Julie: How do you feel about the business that you built?

Gerry: We feel like all that hard work has become a positive perfect storm, in that during the last few years, we've so differentiated ourselves from anybody else in a stagnant economy and with knowledge that our competitors are struggling. We've had growth of over 20 percent a year for the last three or four years. It's rewarding. It's incredibly rewarding. When we first started out, we struggled. It's sort of amazing how much money you can borrow on a credit card when you've had good credit for umpteen years. We had to borrow from our parents. We borrowed from just about every pocket we could find. It was some years ago that we were able to finally repay all the people who helped us, but it took a lot of help financially.

To say it's rewarding, it is. There's obviously the economic success that we appreciate, but our company is a family. Many, many of our employees have been with us for many years. All of our directors and assistant directors have. We like each other, which is good since we spend a lot of time with each other every day. It goes back to the fact that we made a decision to try to meet our mission statement every single day. That mission statement isn't to make money. That mission statement is to provide the highest-quality programs possible to the children and families that we have, and do our best to facilitate the child care experience of our families. It's obviously very difficult to have to go to work and leave your child with someone else.

Julie: Absolutely. When you were going through some of those struggles, what was it that you did, or that you thought, or reinforced each other with?

Gerry: I don't think that was the mindset. It was survival. You just put one foot in front of the other because you've got no choice. You've just got to keep going. Jane has always written the checks, although I am pretty much responsible for everything financial because of my background. During those early years, when we didn't know how we were going to meet each payroll, Jane would just say, "Don't worry. I've got this covered." She was, frankly, lying to me. I guess that was quite a kindness that she did.

Jane: I wouldn't say "lying." I just knew that it was somehow going to work out. One thing that's interesting to me still, fascinating actually, is that after all these years of doing this, we're still learning every day new and better ways to do things. It's never a stagnant experience. It's always a process. Every day I learn something a little bit different and change things up. That makes it interesting too. People ask, "Do you get tired of doing it after all this time?" No, there's never a dull moment.

Julie: Now it's feeling like it's a totally different business than it was when you first started so many years ago?

Jane: Absolutely. And I was a center director for twenty-one years. It wasn't until I opened my fourth center in 2007 that I stopped doing the day-to-day operations of one center, which really meant being there for ten hours a day. That was an interesting experience too, stepping out of that role.

Julie: That must have been a real pivotal point for you where you said, "Okay, I'm going to fully step back so I can get out of the day-to-day director responsibilities."

Jane: It was. I loved being a center director. I thought it was going to be really difficult to step away from it, but that wasn't because I had so many other challenges and so many other things I was working on. I thought I was going to really, really miss that. But it was a pretty easy transition.

Julie: That's why I think a lot of people get stagnant and don't grow, because they don't want to let go of all those responsibilities and duties that are so familiar, and the situations. How did you mentally take that leap? Were there support systems that you used? Is it just that you knew something inside yourself, that you had to go to a different level with your life? What was it that drove that decision for you?

Jane: It was that I didn't have the time to oversee what was going on at the other programs. It was when we built our facility in Simsbury. That was the first time we built a building from the ground up. It was a huge undertaking, and it was impossible for me to do that, oversee the other two centers and run the center I was running. Our children all went through the center. It was a point that they were getting a little bit older, so I was able to take the leap from that too.

Strategy 1
Let go.

Julie: How was that process for you? Were you able to let go and just jump back quickly, or was it a migration into the new role?

Gerry: You let go right away.

Jane: I think I let go right away. You might have the people who took over for me say I didn't, but I'm not much of a control freak. I think I was able to step back pretty easily from that. I never missed getting those five o'clock calls in the morning from people telling me they weren't coming into work.

Julie: So you were okay with releasing that responsibility.

Jane: Absolutely.

Strategy 2
Learn every day.

Gerry: I'd like to affirm something that Jane said. I'm particularly intrigued that she said it, because I don't think I've ever thought of it that way. We do still learn every day. It is absolutely unbelievable. I stopped long ago thinking we know it all. I don't even think we're close. There were periods when I thought, *We've got this nailed.* That was just ridiculous.

Jane: I never thought that.

Gerry: With all those hours we put in, and we've had the benefit of working with people like you, and working with people all over the country, and sharing ideas. It never stops. It's every aspect of the business. It's not just the business portion, but it's how to improve our programs, motivate our staff and interact with our families. It is always a challenge.

Julie: This is a big success secret that got revealed. Whether you have one center, two centers, three centers or a vision for fifteen, the big key is that you never stop learning. Never, ever think you know it all, because people at all different levels of success are always emptying their cups, so that they can fill them with new knowledge and different ideas and different strategies that work. That's a very profound thing you just shared with us: Never stop learning. Always empty out that cup. Know that there are different ways that you can explore to do different things.

It's great to see, because we're going to get to how it is working together as husband and wife. It sounds like you guys have a good balance in place.

Strategy 3

Open your mind to what you can learn from others.

Gerry: We like each other a lot, which is really good.

Julie: I hear that. What Gerry and Jane are saying about themselves and their staff, I've seen it firsthand. When I've been there onsite, I can tell how much everybody really enjoys being together and working there. That's what makes you special in itself.

Gerry: First of all, you absolutely need two things to be able to make it happen. One, you really do have to like each other, and two, you have to have a great deal of respect for each other. That, above all, we do. Any discussion is based on a knowledge that the other person is as smart as you are, and between the two of you you're going to come up with a better idea, usually. That's pretty much how I would characterize a husband-wife team and how it's been working for us. I know when I was in insurance, I was traveling all the time. Jane carried most of the burden of raising our kids when they were young. The last thirteen years have been the best of my life. That perfect storm that put me out of business is the best thing that ever happened to me.

Julie: I just got chills when you shared that. Jane, what makes the business partnership work for you?

Jane: I guess what's nice for me is that we do have a really, really good balance in terms of what Gerry's strengths are and what my strengths are. A lot of it just organically came out of what he was going to be doing and what I'm doing. It was interesting because, even though Gerry had been around the periphery of the business, he really had no idea what was involved in running a child care program. I think that was a real learning experience for him too. I think being the director of a center has got to be one of the most complex and difficult jobs in the world. There are so many skills you have to have. I think that was really eye-opening for him, because he didn't quite get that at first.

Gerry: Not only eye-opening, but eye-opening in the perspective of having run corporations with all sorts of fancy people. I would agree, the job of a child care director exceeds almost any job except the CEO of a large company.

Julie: I always feel that way whenever I work with our directors. It's almost like you are the owner. You are the sole operator. It's like it's their business or their center. There is a lot of ownership and respon-sibility that comes with that management position.

Gerry: If there isn't, then they're not the right person for the job.

Julie: Right. Are there any things you had to purposely talk about, like, "We have to put strategy in place for this, so that we can be suc-cessful as a husband-wife team"? Were there any boundaries that you put in place, or anything that really hung you up, over these several years?

Jane: We do talk about work a lot. For a while I tried to put more of a boundary between us, that on the weekends we're not going to talk about this. That didn't work. Occasionally one of us will say, "Can we just not talk about work anymore?" That doesn't happen very often, I don't think.

Gerry: It happens most every day at about five thirty in the after-noon, but our days start at six o'clock in the morning.

Strategy 4
You are your business.

Julie: I think when your business is your baby, it is something that you gave birth to and you're maturing with and growing. It's a lot to be excited about. I think sometimes it's hard to shut that off.

Jane: It absolutely is. It's pretty all-encompassing.

Gerry: It's not our business. It's our life. It unequivocally is every-thing. Now we're starting to deal with issues of "Where do we want to go with this? Do we want to raise some capital? We're already committed to three additional locations, and two of those should be breaking ground within the next month. What next?" One thing we know is, as long as we own the business, we're in the business and we are the business.

Julie: Especially when you're really successful in a child care business, it is you. I know my business wouldn't be here if I was not in it. Any other things you'd like to add about being a husband-wife team? If someone were to come to you and say, "Jane, Gerry, I really need some advice. I'm thinking about pulling my hubby or wife into this business with me," what would you tell them?

Gerry: We have some friends from around the country who have expressed an interest in sort of following in the footsteps, but struggling because the business isn't generating enough income to offset the husband's—as it happens, that's the way it is—current income. We understand that it can be very difficult for people to take that route. I don't have an answer for that. Somehow you just have to navigate the waters. If you're doing it so you can stand in place, that's probably not going to be something that's going to work. Jane and I know people in Connecticut who stand in place. There are barriers to having it happen. The biggest one is economic.

Jane: I think that's true too. We've also talked to a lot of people who, even if it's not a husband and wife working together yet, are struggling financially. I think that's sometimes because they step out of the director position before they really can afford to do that.

Gerry: Good point.

Jane: To have to pay that salary for a director before you're financially able to do that sometimes can be a big error that people make early on.

Julie: So giving up that role too early.

Gerry: Jane, that's a great point, by the way.

Strategy 5

Make everything ducky.

Julie: Tell us about the ducks in your logo. Why are those important to you?

Jane: A friend of mine from college was working in a public relations firm in Manhattan. He did logo work, and I just asked him to come up with a design. That's what he came up with, sort of the momma duck looking after the little ducks behind her.

Gerry: It's been fun because we're able to make everything ducky. Whether it's the Ducky Bucks we give our employees or the Duck Bunch, the name of one of our programs, it's fun being able to throw the ducks into all sorts of stuff.

Julie: I still have my duck hat that you gave me, and I love wearing it.

Gerry: We have a duck mascot costume, which is fun. Both males and females have worn the costume. They've been able to meet other mascots around the state, like the local baseball team's.

Julie: I think that's an important thing to pay attention to. You want something that makes you different so you can get those press releases, so you can get some attention to your child care program.

Jane: I know one thing that was important in choosing the name and logo—I didn't want something that looked silly and childish. That was sort of what many of the day care centers around were doing, or funky spelling of words. I really wanted to try to start out with a more professional image.

Gerry: It's really a traditional symbol with the mother and the ducks following, like, "Make way for ducklings." We were just in Boston and took a picture of something in a park there with a mother duck followed by all the baby ducks, just as cute as you can imagine. It certainly reflects the caring and maternal aspects of child care.

Julie: Absolutely. I've seen that in action with the ducks, when the mom won't leave the pond or land until all the ducklings are in and safe with her. They are spectacular to watch. I think in Boston there's a statute too, isn't there?

Jane: Yes.

Julie: What else makes you different? When you think about this entity you've created and what really sets you apart, what are some of those things?

Strategy 6
Don't deny requests for supplies.

Gerry: Like I said, I think our focus has never been on making money. It was sort of, "If we build it, they will come," as the phrase from the movie goes, where he built a ballpark and the players came out from the shadows. We've just been of the belief that if we meet our mission statement, and work every day toward being the best, then success would follow. At least for now it seems like that's been a good equation to follow. We haven't been foolish. For example, we now have employee orientation every month. It's three hours on the first Saturday of the month. One of the things I tell our employees is, "I don't want to ever, ever hear, when we do an employee questionnaire, that you don't have adequate supplies." We haven't turned down a supply request in memory. We have certain rules like, "You can't buy things that have batteries," but those rules are few. When we've looked at the financial equation, supplies are such a small portion of the total that we're not going to cut corners there. That applies to our interest in providing our staff with the most comprehensive benefits we can. Right up and down the line, it's been that we're not going to make money by watching every penny. Again, that's not to say that we're idiots or foolish. We obviously do try to manage staff hours, for example, but not at the cost of the quality of our programs. That would be true of every single item on the balance sheet.

Strategy 7
Staff is your foundation.

Jane: Even going all the way back to the very beginning, when no child care centers were offering any benefits, I offered health insurance. People weren't giving their employees vacation days, paid sick days or anything else. I really think the foundation for everything we do is the staff we have. A child care program is nothing without its staff. We've always really tried to provide the best working environment for them and the best benefits that we can. Certainly the most important thing in the child care center, I think, is the director of the program. We are very fortunate to have a truly wonderful, talented group of directors and assistant directors.

Strategy 8
Pour your passion into your business.

Julie: I know in creating our own businesses, we have the opportunity to let our businesses reflect some of who we are. We can incorporate our passions into our profession, which makes us unique, which makes us different. I think there are some things that you guys are passionate about that you've incorporated into your business, into what you offer parents and into what makes you stand out in the community. I know there are things like having minimally processed foods and healthy eating. Jane, from what I know, I think that's probably a personal passion of yours.

Jane: We've always provided lunch and snacks and had kitchens at all of our facilities, which is unusual for around here. When I first started, it was the middle of the 1980s, and we had, for a long time, a completely vegetarian diet at the centers, which was very popular at that point. Then later it became less popular. We've always emphasized good nutrition. We did just newly refocus on that. Also, physical fitness—we've never used videos or sedentary activities. A lot of the other programs in the area were having children sit in front of the TV for part of the day. We've tried to promote healthy habits from the beginning.

Strategy 9
Implement new ideas.

Gerry: In the broader sense, there are people who just laugh at us when I go to some of our meetings where we meet with other child care owners. If there's a good idea, we are jumping up and down and doing it ten minutes later. It's a long list. What's happened, certainly here in Connecticut, is we seem to be the only ones who are doing that, who are constantly differentiating. It's not like we even need to anymore. On our website, we actually have "What Makes Us Different." Program after program is listed there. Whether it's our infant sign language that we include for all, or the fact we include kinder music and yoga in our curriculum for everyone, and we have an exercise and fitness program, and on and on. We could stop now and say we're doing great. If I hear, or Jane hears, a great idea tomorrow, we're doing it. Jane and I founded the Connecticut Child Care Association last year. We're up to about one hundred fifty members and two hundred fifty programs, which is, by the way, about 25 percent of the state, because we are small. We have an opportunity to speak to other child care owners continuously. Right now it's eating up a huge amount of time. What I'm saying is, our mindset is different. It seems that their mindset is managing their day-to-day problems, as opposed to having a mindset of *What can I do to get even better today?*

Julie: That's huge. I hope everybody is writing that down. What makes you different is: Are you managing by problems, or are you managing by a bigger vision that you have for what you can incorporate?

Jane: The other thing I started focusing on was I really wanted to make the child care experience a good experience for the entire family. I realized that when I was the mother of three very young children, who were all coming to work with me. Gerry was traveling all the time. What I decided to do at that point was to put some things into the day at the center so the parents wouldn't have to be driving the kids around on the weekends and nights and taking away from family time. We started doing things like having somebody come in once a month to offer haircuts at the center. We started doing extracurricular activities during the day, so kids could go to dance lessons from our center. We would transport them back and forth to gymnastics, and that type of thing. I knew, as a very, very busy mom of little kids whose husband was traveling a lot, that that was incredibly helpful for us. We've continued and grown in all those extra services we provide.

Julie: I think that's something that parents highly value, their time. That's fantastic that you're offering those services.

Gerry: We have a family meal night. We've been through a number of providers. We seem to have finally hit on a very successful formula with the restaurant we're working with now. Parents can order food on Monday or Tuesday and pick it up at the center on Thursday. It's very affordable, huge portions, delicious. Basically they either have to microwave it or put it in the oven for twenty minutes. They have a restaurant-quality meal with many kid-friendly selections. Not everyone uses it, but the ones who do, love it. I'd probably say 10 to 20 percent of our families use it.

Julie: I would love it—get my hair cut, meals done. Do you guys do dry cleaning too?

Jane: We did that for a while. We did dry cleaning drop-off and pick-up. We've had some things we've done that have not been a success. We'll try anything. I think the parents do really, more than anything, appreciate having some time back with their families.

Strategy 10
Identify what doesn't work.

Julie: Can you share with us a couple of things you tried that weren't so successful?

Jane: The dry cleaning was one.

Gerry: A parents' night out never worked.

Jane: Parents have frequently said, "Can you please offer a Saturday of care, right before Christmas for shopping?" No one ever comes. We did a parents' night out where the kids could stay and have dinner and games and crafts. That's another thing that parents loved the idea of, but when we've offered it, it's never been successful. I think sometimes they like the idea of things more than they like the actuality. We do a lot of social activities for the families. We have cookouts and potlucks and that sort of thing. Those are very popular.

Gerry: Those are very popular, but they've been very difficult to do. When we had more energy, we used to do a spaghetti night or something.

Jane: We used to do that with the different classrooms.

Gerry: They loved it, but it honestly became too much, with the demands that we have during the seven-to-six hours that we're open. As much as we would like to, every month, have the parents have an opportunity to talk to each other, that was something I would put in the category of wildly successful but just . . .

Jane: That was also something that when I was the center director there, and our kids were there, it was an easy and fun thing to do, but it would be a lot to ask the directors to do on a regular basis. They've got their own lives and families to get home to. My life and my family were there, so it didn't make any difference.

Julie: One of the things that parents often ask about when they're looking for quality child care is motivated staff. Everybody in the child care industry pretty much wonders, *How do we have motivated staff?* I heard Gerry's voice light up when he talked about these Ducky Bucks for staff. Can you share with us a little bit about what Ducky Bucks are? I'm sure that's one of the things that makes you different and helps your team feel good and positive about where they work.

Gerry: First we need to give credit where credit is due. We stole that from Rochelle Kiner and The Oxford School in Columbus, Ohio. She calls them Oxford Bucks.

Julie: We've been talking about them ourselves for years. I'm sure there are all sorts of adaptations of them.

Gerry: I think the book is still open on how we gauge the program. We started it four or five months ago. The idea is that when someone does something above and beyond—if they stay late, take out the trash, just anything at all—they can earn a Ducky Buck or two. Teachers can nominate each other. We set up a sliding scale of rewards where they can trade those in for gift cards, or even vacation days. We just had our first teacher turn them in. I think she used about fifty or sixty Ducky Bucks to get a vacation day.

Jane: I think people like them.

Strategy 11

Reward the good.

Julie: So often leaders, owners and directors get caught up in extensively focusing on the things that aren't working. The people who are not doing the right things in your organization tend to get all the attention.

Jane: That's absolutely true.

Julie: Ducky Bucks are a way to say, "Okay, we're going to step out and recognize those who are doing the right thing, so we're giving our attention there." What you give energy to is typically what grows.

Gerry: Another thing we've done in the last year: We went through this exercise called Shoves and Tugs. We found it in a book we particularly liked.

Jane: *The Deadly Sins of Employee Retention*.

Gerry: We had our directors sit down with each staff member and say, "What's keeping you here, and what's pushing you away?" The idea was, *Let's let our hair down and be honest. If we've got problems,* *let's discuss them and see what we can do.* From talking to our directors, that's been a very positive experience for them, and the employees as well.

Jane: It's also a sort of shift in thinking and looking at it and saying, "Not all turnover is bad turnover. If we can improve people's performance, great, but if we can't, then maybe there are some people who it's better for them to exit. Let's really focus on our great employees." The same things don't motivate everyone. Different people are motivated by different things. You have to figure out what that is, if you're going to motivate your staff.

Gerry: In that same context, we actually went through a formal process. We have a human resources consultant who is with us part time. He went to each of our directors and asked them to rate each one of their employees as a 1, 2 or 3. Then he said, "You can't have all 1's, so I want that evenly distributed by thirds." Then Jane and I sort of got involved. We said, "The people who are 1's, let's recognize them. The people who are 2's, let's tell them what they need in order to be a 1. The people who are 3's, let's tell them they're a 3." I don't mean tell them they're a number, but sit down with them and say, "You're not meeting our expectations. Here's what you're going to have to do. If you're not going to do this, you're not going to have a job." We've taken a very proactive stance toward improving the quality of our staff. Those 3's are pulling down the 1's.

Julie: I think that's critical. That's missing from a lot of child care programs, just sitting down with your staff and having those one-on-one discussions. So often we want to do it through a general memo or some other way. There is nothing so transformational and powerful as sitting down one-on-one and letting them know directly where these improvements need to happen. I agree with that. Great strategy.

Jane: It was really interesting too, because then the directors realized which people were underperforming. A lot of the staff had no idea they weren't doing what they were supposed to be doing. It's helped overall, an awful lot.

Julie: Awareness is key. Anything you can do to bring awareness to a situation is going to help that situation change.

Jane: I think most people want to do a good job. Nobody thinks, *I'm going to go to work today and do a crummy job.*

Julie: *I want to go to work today, feel horrible about where I work, go home stressed out, not want to go back tomorrow and not want to get a paycheck.* It's true. This is what I've found in my work with teams over the past thirteen years. Most people are good staff, and they want to do better, it's just that they need help in making that leap to get there. Sometimes directors, leaders and owners don't know how to get them there. Having that one-on-one communication is a powerful start. I know you've done a lot of marketing. What do you think is the most powerful way you get new, dreamy clients in through your doors?

Strategy 12

Keep your online presence strong.

Gerry: We have a very expensive website. Getting people to go to that website would rank way high. We have an unlimited budget for our Google AdWords, and we do SEO, search engine optimization. The key to getting that person to dial the phone in the first place, it's the website and getting them there online. Obviously, it's word of mouth. They're put in the funnel, as we've been taught to think. We place emphasis on everything from how you handle the initial phone call, with an emphasis on getting that person to come in and see how wonderful you are, to staying in contact with them—for which we use our lead management system CRM, and communicating with them constantly until they become a lost opportunity—and our focus on how to give a tour.

There's no single thing. This has been a building process of basically focusing on every aspect of our business. Then, when we get them in, keeping them happy. What do you do so that they don't leave? Obviously that's by doing what you say you're going to do, following up, giving them a call after their first week, giving them another call at the end of the month. These are all procedures that we've put in place. It's a never-ending process, from the day somebody Googles us, or the day somebody's friend refers them and they come in. There are just so many other pieces to this. If you walk into one of our foyers, you'll see this computer screen that is constantly rotating the pictures of the children that we sent out just that day to the parents. We send out pictures every day to the parents, of the children engaged in activities. It's a myriad of things.

Jane: I think the other thing is, we realized a couple of years ago that our directors really were not focusing on enrollment. They didn't want to be too salesy or pushy. We don't want them being too pushy, but we spent a whole lot of time with directors and assistant directors talking about how important getting the enrollment is.

Gerry: Let me put it a different way. We honestly do think we're the best. The mindset that we wanted to give our directors when they give a tour is that it would be a disservice for that child not to come to Educational Playcare. It's your job to tell them why that's the case.

Julie: That's a big success secret in itself, to have the mindset that you are the best, and to be able to stand with confidence in that. I think that sets you apart, in and of itself. There are so many people on shaky grounds like, *Are we really the best?* They know they're not doing everything they can do to serve their clients right. So really stand in that power, and know that you are the best in this industry. Let's give a final list of three success strategies that you would say you have to do to be a successful child care business. What would those things be?

Gerry: I'm going to start with an easy one. You have to understand that the commitment to success is all-encompassing. It really is 24/7/365. Maybe for us it's 12/7/365. Without that commitment—all the stuff we've been babbling about on the phone the last hour—it's not possible, at least to the extent that we've been successful at Educational Playcare. There needs to be an understanding of the type of commitment that's required, and in this case, it's been two of us. When we talk to other child care centers and there's an individual owner, we know it's been such a huge advantage for us. We've been able to double that commitment. That would be my first comment. If you don't understand what that commitment is, and if you're starting from scratch, you need to understand that this isn't going to happen overnight. It's a long process, and it's all-consuming.

Jane: Another thing I would say is you have to be completely committed to having a high-quality program, and a program that's really good for the children and their parents. Some people go into it simply as a business, and aren't really committed to child care in itself. I think it's really important to start with that as your mission, to provide a good, quality program for the children, rather than to start as being a successful business. They go hand in hand.

Gerry: The third thing is, if you don't like what you're doing, it's not going to happen. You really have to look at yourself and say, "What makes me happy?" I think that this process has been so fulfilling. The success is really nice, but the process itself—I think both Jane and I are people who thrive on the day-to-day learning.

Update: Educational Playcare was named a Hartford (Connecticut) Courant Top Workplace 2016. Companies made the list based on surveys about the workplace, completed by their employees. Additionally, Educational Playcare now has fifteen centers, with the additional locations in Berlin, Cheshire, Glastonbury, Madison, Mansfield, Oxford and Windsor-West. One West Hartford location has grown to two: West Hartford on Fennway and West Hartford on Park.

To hear this interview in its entirety, go to **www.ChildCareBusinessSuccess BookVault.com**. The password is **RockMyChildCare.com**.

Chapter 6

WOW! A Waiting List

Featuring Carolyn Driggers,
Appletree Child Development Center

"One of the great lessons of effective marketing is frequency and consistency. Companies that struggle usually 'turn on' their marketing only when sales slow down. Thriving companies recognize the need to consistently and persistently be in front of customers and prospects."

Jim Palmer

*I*t's all about word of mouth. It's all about building relationships. It's all about having your dream team in place. Carolyn Driggers, owner of Appletree Day Care, credits these factors for the success that she's enjoying in her child care business.

The business of child care is one that she fell quickly in love with while working in her family's real estate business. I recently had the opportunity to visit each one of Carolyn's four centers in Raleigh, North Carolina, and see her face light up as she watched the children play, learn, nap and eat. And even more so was the joy in her face when she saw her incredibly talented staff in action. Like many child care programs, hers has an artist, a gymnast and song writer on her team. Oh, and I'll never forget Mr. John, who is the program's bus driver; during a team retreat that I facilitated for Carolyn, it was clear through his powerful and dynamic presence that he has natural talents in public speaking.

Carolyn got into the child care field when she was expecting her second child. She was working in her family's real estate business at the time and noticed that there weren't any quality child care facilities where she wanted to send her own children. Then a building she was dealing with through the real estate business became vacant, and she thought it would be a great location for a child care center. Her ideas and vision started to come to life. But unfortunately she was met with doubt and discouragement, as her father dissuaded her for a while. As time went on and the building continued to sit vacant, he had a change of heart. He encouraged her to open a child care center—but insisted she hire a director to run it so that she could continue in the family real estate business. He didn't want to lose her! So she followed his desires. She opened the child care program and hired a director. Then, as fate happened, she spent some vacation time away from her real estate job working hands-on in the child care center, and quickly fell in love with the staff, the children and the parents. Soon afterward she became the facility director, and she's never looked back. Now, she's following her desires and celebrating twenty-four years of child care business success! Even though she has a director at each center, she stills remains actively involved with the operations and activities at each of her four locations.

Julie: One of the reasons we asked Carolyn to be in this interview series with us is because she's somebody who's really committed to making her business better and better every single year. This, to you, Carolyn, must have felt like a real journey over the past twenty-four years.

Carolyn: It's been a journey. I think we're finally where I want to be. We're doing things the right way, I believe, now. I look forward to it each and every day, to see what we can do bigger and better.

Julie: If you could go back twenty-four years, and say, "If I knew then what I know now," what would some of those things be? These could be challenges that you overcame, challenges you're still facing, successes. We always have that retrospective look, where we look back and say, "If only I knew these things when I first started."

Strategy 1

Build brand recognition.

Carolyn: I think when you first start, it just takes a while to get your name out there. Establishing good rapport with the parents we've had has helped me so much along the way. I've relied most of my business on word of mouth. What I would have done differently is now I'm doing a whole lot more advertising. I believe with having my brand already out there, and then doing the advertising that I'm doing now, we could have had a waiting list ten years ago. That's one thing I really would have done differently.

Julie: So getting your brand out there and doing some advertising. When it comes to advertising and establishing your brand, what are some of the things that you think are the most critical, and that have served you well, when it comes to you being successful?

Carolyn: What's serving me well right now is that we have our name out there in the movie theater. When families go to the movies, they see our commercial. We're also on a TV station. I do radio advertising and also put out flyers. By being in the community for twenty-four years, we've just got that reputation, and people are recognizing us because we've been doing the advertising for quite some time now.

Julie: That's fantastic. When you think about your branding, do you think about a logo, or do you think about a consistency in message? Do you think about colors? What do you think is the most critical piece of that puzzle for you?

Carolyn: Definitely the logo. The website is a tremendous help. I get so many referrals from my website. I went for years not having one. Now that I have one, that's generating a lot of business for me. That really helps. Having the same logo out there on your business card, on your vehicles, and through everything, people see it all the time and share it with others. That has, I believe, really helped my business today.

Julie: I like what you're saying. I think a lot of people don't realize how valuable of a space their vehicles are when it comes to positioning your logo or your company name.

Carolyn: We have our vehicles out there on the road every day, going to several schools. Parents picking up their kids at the schools see it if they need child care. Or just going down the road, if they're expecting, or know somebody who's going to be having, a baby, they can let them know they saw the vehicle on the road. That does help.

Julie: I think it's invaluable. When I was first speaking, marketing experts would tell us, "If you write any books, stick them in the back window of your car, so people can go by and see your book—or your card for what you're doing—right there in the rear window.

They say, "Take your car to book stores, here and there. Let people walk by and see it, because that helps with that brand recognition and visibility." Do you think the signs that you have on your vehicles should be high-end to start off with?

Carolyn: No. They can even be magnetic, and stick them on. People just need to see your name and your logo on it. Ours are painted on, but you can start out simple, as long as people are seeing it.

Julie: That's fantastic. One of the questions that people in this industry want to know the answer to is, "What makes you different? What do you think sets you apart from any other child care program that's out there?"

Strategy 2

Be invested in your business.

Carolyn: I think one thing that sets Appletree apart from some others is that we are locally owned and operated. I'm invested in the business each and every day. I know what's going on at all the facilities. We are moving more toward social media. We have Facebook, but a lot of child care programs do not have that. We're just now getting into electronic daily grams versus giving handwritten notes each and every day, and the parents say, "I didn't know my child didn't have diapers," or something like that. This way, it goes out to them electronically. It lets them know that their child needs diapers, and what all the children did during the day, plus they get pictures of their children. What parent doesn't enjoy pictures of their child and seeing them throughout the day? Then they get a picture sent to them during the day at work, to their cell phone, and they get to show their co-workers. When they're showing their co-worker that, not only is the co-worker seeing a picture of their child, but they're seeing our brand. Again, our logo and our name are on the electronic daily gram that goes out.

Julie: It's so true. What do people do when they go out to dinner at night, or they get together at functions, or even when they first meet somebody? They pull out their cell phone and say, "Look at the pictures of my kids!"

Carolyn: We're going to be sending out two pictures per day. There are an average of twenty-one school days per month. That's a lot of pictures that they're getting per month, which they can share with their relatives who live out of state, or something like that. They get to see pictures of their children growing up, while they may not take as many at home.

Julie: Very true. So you're creating these long-lasting memories for parents to capture, that they'll have forever. That's wonderful. Where did it begin for you? Why did you get into this industry?

Carolyn: I got into child care when I was expecting my second child. I was looking around for child care, and I just really did not see any quality child care facilities in the area. I happened to be in real estate at the time, working for a family business. We had a building go vacant. I said, "That would make a great location for child care." Of course, my dad said, "No, you're not opening up a child care." Well, the building sat vacant, and next thing I knew, he came to me and said, "You're going to open up a child care, but you're not going to run it. You're going to hire a director." I said, "Okay." I started doing that, and then I came up on my vacation time, took my vacation at the child care, fell in love with the staff and fell in love with the children and parents. I didn't feel like enough children were coming in quickly enough, so I got rid of the director and ran it from then on out, and never went back to the family business of real estate. I love it.

Julie: You found it was best to be hands-on with the directing of your center.

Carolyn: Exactly. That's what got us started. We started off small, and the next thing I knew I was able to open up another center. Then years later I opened another, then my fourth location. Just the love that I have for the children, just to watch them grow, is amazing. Now the children I used to care for years ago are bringing me their children. The only place they want them to be is Appletree, because that's where they went. That makes it wonderful.

Julie: Which may explain why now you have a waiting list.

Carolyn: Correct.

Julie: That's fantastic. What was going through your mind? At the time you were running one, you were successful with that first location. What were some of the thoughts you were weighing when it came to, *Do I want to have a second location?*

Strategy 3
Take a risk.

Carolyn: At that time we had just outgrown our building, and we were full. A building came available right across the street. I decided to separate it, and make one for infants and toddlers, and one for preschool. We were just doing pretty good. I said, "Let me go for a larger center." I took over an existing center, and things went well there. One thing developed into the other. I really enjoy the business aspect, seeing if I can do that. I like a challenge. I guess the hardest thing is to make sure all four centers are doing the same thing and representing the company altogether, versus one being

127

different. That's my biggest challenge, making sure they're all on the same page. When you want quality, you want all four to be the same.

Julie: Kind of like I love going to Marriott because I know what I can expect. I know I'm going to have the Marriott experience.

Carolyn: And no matter which Marriott, you're getting the same service.

Julie: Right, getting pretty much the same thing. So it was just a matter of "We're growing, we need to be bigger, so why not"?

Carolyn: Yes.

Julie: Then were there any other thoughts that came into your mind, when it came to opening the third and fourth locations?

Carolyn: I guess the challenges we've run into are with staffing—making sure you get quality staff in there. Staying in touch with parents is great. They're still our best advertisers. I guess staffing would be one of the issues.

Julie: So staffing still comes up as something that's challenging? We hear that a lot, that staffing is the biggest issue. Were there any things you were trying to weigh out when it came to really getting to the point where you were opening your fourth center, or was it that you felt you were just growing and it was time to expand?

Carolyn: I've had people ask me all the time, and I get calls from people, "Do you want to open up another center?" I don't. I'm comfortable right now with where I want to be. I don't want to be too large, where I can't manage them all. To me, opening a fifth location is not what I want to do, because I like being involved and having the closeness with all the families at all the locations. I don't want to lose that.

Julie: Let's talk about the name Appletree. Where did that come from?

Carolyn: The first location had fruit trees in the back of the property, and several of them were apple trees. I wanted to be in the A's to be at the beginning of the phonebook. Back then, everybody went to phonebooks.

Julie: Everybody was ABC Company or AAA.

Carolyn: You didn't do Internet and things like that, so I wanted to be one of the first listings in the Yellow Pages. I went for A and called it Appletree.

Julie: And it has stuck.

Carolyn: It has stuck. Yes, it has.

Julie: I'm sure in the past twenty-four years you have heard many comments from parents about your child care program, the difference that you make, the difference that the teachers in your program make. Is there one thing that is just a really profound memory to you, in terms of how much of an impact you do have on the children's lives?

Carolyn: I guess the biggest impact would be what we're going through now, when the children that I did keep are coming back and saying they want their children in there. They don't want their children to go to any other center, because that's where they grew up. Then seeing what those children are doing today, that's just very rewarding and makes it wonderful.

Julie: That's the biggest thing you like to hear, "I don't want my kid to go anywhere else except here, Appletree, where I went."

Carolyn: Exactly.

Julie: What's one of your passions as a child care business owner? What part of running your child care program is it that you really love?

Strategy 4
Really like the business part of child care.

Carolyn: I like the business aspect, seeing what I can do for the center, for the company as a whole, what I can do for the teachers, what I can give back to their classrooms that's going to help the children to nurture and grow. Children are just so smart. Their minds are like sponges. They absorb so much. We want to have all those opportunities in the classroom for them to learn and grow.

Julie: You were telling me that one of the things you love are the numbers. Sometimes people are afraid to look at the numbers and embrace the numbers. Tell me what your numbers, and knowing your numbers, has meant to you as a child care business owner.

Carolyn: I keep up with the business with QuickBooks. Most people have a monthly budget that they follow. My numbers have always been in the targeted range of what we're supposed to be for payroll and things like that. They just automatically turn over into that. It's not something that I've studied a whole lot, and I wish I had more time for that. My favorite thing is putting everything together to see how we're doing, opening a new center and being in the positive the first year, versus being in the red. So many businesses are in the red. They struggle to operate that first year. It's nice having that challenge and the rewarding experience that we did it.

Julie: Seeing those numbers being a reflection of your business success is probably pretty awesome.

Carolyn: Yes, it is.

Julie: If you had an opportunity to do anything else besides child care, would you take that opportunity?

Carolyn: No. I love what I do. Every day is different. With the changing times and everything, I've learned so much in the past five years, with the advertising and going out on a different branch, where I would never have done that before. It's still rewarding. It's still challenging. I'm still learning new things.

Julie: I think that's a big success tip, to keep learning new things. Never think you know everything. Some of my top clients are successful because they keep emptying their cup. They keep saying, "Show me more, show me better, show me different."

Carolyn: Yes.

Julie: That's wonderful. You also attribute a lot of your success to the positive word of mouth that comes in from the community. Is there anything that you think helps that? I know we could look at advertising and what's on cars, but I think it takes a little bit more than that—deeper relationships that you have with people in the community, or just people who are out there who are your raving fans. What do you think it is that really helps drive that positive word of mouth for you, so that you're getting a lot of that referral business?

Strategy 5

Building proactive relationships goes a long way.

Carolyn: Being there for your families, making sure you're greeting them in the morning. Always have a smile on your face. They don't have to know that you're five teachers short and don't know how you're going to do the lunch schedule that day. The important thing is to hold your head up high, smile and greet them. Let them know that they are important.

Julie: I love that. I always remember Mary Kay Ash's quote—she's the founder of Mary Kay Cosmetics. "Pretend that every single person you meet has a sign hanging around his or her neck that says, 'Make me feel important.' Not only will you succeed in sales, you will succeed in life." I never forget that quote. That just gives testimonial to the power of it. So making them feel important and being there to greet them.

Carolyn: That's absolutely important. They want to know that you're there and that you care.

Julie: Relationships are really important to you. Are there any success strategies that you can share about things you do during tours, or when you get parents on the phone, to build those positive relationships?

Carolyn: One thing that our company has started doing within the past two years, and I do believe that this also contributes to us now having a waiting list and having so many people to tour our center, is that we use ChildCareCRM. When potential clients call in, we get all the pertinent information we need to plug into the software. Then we send them an inquiry packet that has all of our information in it. After that, we send another e-mail asking them to schedule a tour. We like to have scheduled tours when they come by, because that gives us that time we can dedicate, forty-five minutes to an hour, to help them feel comfortable, to show them all of our facility and to answer any questions they may have. After they leave, they also get a follow-up e-mail: Thank you for touring. There are about six e-mails that go out just from that one phone call. That way, they know that you're up on technology, and they know more about your program than the child care down the street that they visited.

Julie: So it's really a way to nurture those relationships and set yourself apart. ChildCareCRM is great. It's actually one of the sponsors of our *Child Care Business Success* book and of this teleseminar series. We think Chuck Gibbs and ChildCareCRM are awesome.

Carolyn: They're wonderful. That has helped a whole lot, and the parents really like it too. Especially with parents today, they're so tech-savvy. They just really enjoy it.

Julie: Does the communication from ChildCareCRM go to their cell phones too?

Carolyn: Yes.

Julie: There have been studies done showing that cell phones are only five feet away from us at all times, anywhere we go, twenty-four hours a day. What a powerful way to market, by being able to get that communication to a parent over the telephone.

Carolyn: And it's important, when they do come in for the tour, that they see your whole program. Even if they have a three-year-old, you want to start off making sure they do see the infant room. Down the road, they may have an infant. We want them to see all the classrooms and all the playgrounds.

Julie: You never know when they might need a service that you have to offer, and they need to know about all those things.

Carolyn: Yes, they do.

Julie: What about other involvement in the community? Is there anything else that you do to nurture relationships, or build relationships, with people who are in your area?

Carolyn: We do some things like during Halloween, we go to the museum and pass out candy with our information on it. A TV station sponsors that. So when the parents get home, they see a brochure or business card and our logo and contact information on the candy that they received. That helps get our name out there. Also, we're giving their child candy when they come, so they're going to a safe place. Then there's Family Fest, sponsored by a radio station and TV station. That's at one of our local parks. There are a lot of people out there, and we're advertising there as well.

Julie: That sounds like a lot of fun too.

Strategy 6
Become part of a community of owners who are committed to success.

Carolyn: I think it's important in meeting with other providers in other states, finding groups like yours, Julie, getting into groups where you can hear other people's ideas and what's worked for them and what hasn't, and just share things. That's been very rewarding for me lately. I guess it's gotten me to think outside the box. I think that's where I have the advantage right now, versus my competitors in the area. It gets me to go out and find out new ideas, and then I can come back and develop those for my company and what works for me. Not every idea you hear is going to work, but if you walk away with three ideas your company can use, it's so worth it. Meeting other providers gives you another resource pool, because you can call them if you ever need a suggestion or anything like that.

Julie: You're building up that network. I'm going to be very bold and make a statement here. I'm going to be writing an article about this soon, because I really believe this. A lot of time, as directors or owners, we think there's just our immediate community when it comes to going to a director support group or other organizations that are there to support us. They don't necessarily put us in the right mind-set to achieve that child care business success. Sometimes success isn't always the most convenient thing, but it is really important. This was established many years ago in Napoleon Hill's *Think and Grow Rich*, when he talked about having mastermind groups. These are people who really have a desire in their hearts to create successful businesses, who don't want to play into the lack talk they're hearing in little support groups. Kudos to you for taking some steps to find groups that support you. It's not always convenient for you, because you have to travel somewhere. You have to fit it into your schedule. It can be a big, huge leap for you, but that's where you can start making big, huge leaps when it comes to you being successful in your child care business, finding other like-minded people.

Carolyn: And it puts you so far above your competitors, it's unbelievable. Sometimes going out of town can be an inconvenient moment, but what you walk away with from being in a mastermind group for two days is so rewarding. It just rejuvenates you and gives you a clearer mind, so you want to come back and work on your business.

Julie: Absolutely. That's a big thing. Not a lot of child care owners are connecting with other high-level thinkers in the child care industry. I think sometimes in this industry it's like, "A coach, a mastermind group, what's that?" A lot of times local child care groups have a lack mentality and don't challenge owners to expand their mind-sets. When you participate in those kinds of groups, it can crush your ability to function as the visionary for your life (personally and professionally). Be very selective with the people you're hanging around. Will these people propel you to another level of success with your business?

Carolyn: I agree. Meeting mainly with people out of state and not in your area helps your business by far.

Julie: Is there anything you do that you feel really helps parents build trust, even before they come into your program? In addition to the advertising, is there anything you feel you do that inspires parents to sign up with you when they come in for a tour?

Strategy 7
Honesty is the first step in building trust.

Carolyn: My parents know I'm honest with them. Honesty is the best thing. If we're having a problem with one of the rooms, I'm not going to deny it. Be honest with them. Be up front with them. They're going to respect you and stay with you a lot longer.

Julie: Where does setting boundaries come into play? There's always a fine line between building those positive relationships and having good, professional boundaries in place with parents, and then the honesty component. Are there boundaries that you set for yourself, when it comes to your interactions with the parents?

Carolyn: You always keep it professional, not personal. You greet them and everything like that, but you always keep it on a professional level. Let them know you do have a high-quality program. You have to believe in your program, and I believe in my program. It's everything for me. They know that when they've met me and my staff, we do believe in what we're doing and that it is a quality program.

Julie: How do you structure the models that you have in place for your centers? Did you look to somebody else's child care program, or did you just do what you felt fit when you wanted to establish consistency between your four organizations?

Carolyn: When I first started out, it was me creating everything—all of our handbooks (including our employee handbook and our parent handbook). I did everything myself. I guess I learned from the school of hard knocks, being in the business. What I'm learning now that's so rewarding is that, by being in the mastermind groups, I get to find out what's worked for other companies. Then I bring it back to my area and try it at my center. Not everything is going to work. You have to find out what's important for you first. Some of the things I have done have really made a difference to the business.

Julie: Can you share with us a few of the things that you've incorporated into your model for your four programs?

Strategy 8

Develop your processes and procedures.

Carolyn: Bringing LifeCubby in, the electronic daily reports, that's been humongous. I wasn't doing as many mailers, where now I'm doing more mailers. You're not guaranteed tomorrow. I'm now working on putting everything into a manual so that the directors don't have to call me for everything. I can say, "What does Page 24 say? What does Page 295 say?" That way they have a clear understanding, and there are no gray areas. This is the way the owner of the company wants to run it. They have to do things the same. I'm working on my operations manual now. You would think after twenty-four years I would have it, but I don't.

Julie: You're not alone. Even with the calls we get, "How do we get everybody on the same page?" we answer, "What's in your operations manual? Do you have business processes laid out?" There are some quick and easy, dirty ways you can get those done, but the important thing is to start getting them done. Then that book, think about how much that book will be worth. That's like a million-dollar piece of information right there. That does enable you to have freedom as a business owner.

Carolyn: It does. It helps a whole lot, so that you can concentrate more on your business and not be *in* the business as much. I think that's where I have a hard time separating, because I do enjoy being in the business. I enjoy it so much that I just don't want to give up that piece. I know that I need to back away and be more at the corporate office, working on the business and not in it as much.

Julie: It's the way you grow and be successful. Another big thing about that is that's the way you can get to the point where you're taking care of yourself too. I know that a lot of child care business owners tend to put themselves last on the list.

Carolyn: They do. And when you're starting a business, it does take time away from your family. After being in it for twenty-four years, I do need to start giving back to my family for all the times I was gone when I was getting it up and going.

Julie: And yourself. Don't forget about that. Take time for what you enjoy.

Carolyn: That's where those trips come in, and meeting with other masterminders. That's kind of for myself, to clear my head. It gets me away and gets me rejuvenated.

Julie: I love my mastermind groups too. I think regardless of what level you're at in your business, there's always a mastermind group out there that will support you, a group, a coach, someone. Even if you're at the very basic level, there's a very basic-level coach for you. You may outgrow your coach at different times. Then you change coaches, who you're working with. You may have multiple coaches helping you achieve various results. It's a very flexible kind of thing that works for you, when it comes to coaches and masterminds and all that good stuff. You mentioned flyers when you were talking about some of the strategies you were implementing. I know a lot of people out there think, *We've done mailers, and they don't work.* What have you found to be really effective with your mailers?

Strategy 9
Always have a call to action.

Carolyn: Always put in an offer. What we put in ours is two free months. When people bring that in, we take their monthly tuition and multiply it by 10 and divide it by 12. So they're still paying you something every month, even that first month that they're there. The two months free is a huge savings for them. That's money they would have spent anyway that can now go somewhere else. Put in an offer and give an expiration date, so that you can get them to act soon.

Julie: Very true. Those are good things because a lot of people will do flyers where there's no offer, no expiration date, nothing except information "about us."

Carolyn: You have to put an offer on there if you want to get them to respond.

Julie: What is it, as a child care business owner, that brings you absolutely pure joy when it comes to what you have to deal with as an owner?

Carolyn: Pure joy would be being able to see the difference you made in the life of a child, and having a good name for yourself, a positive name.

Julie: I know a lot of our owners will say, "We have kids who come back, and it's the most gratifying thing. Or even just seeing the kids run up to you in the morning and they're happy to see you."

Carolyn: It is, no matter what kind of day you're having. Even if you're having a bad day, you can't let the parent know that, can't let the child know that. Just to get down and get that hug from that kid is rewarding.

Strategy 10

Keep people who are in line with your vision. Stop tolerating the others.

Julie: Have you ever had to fire a parent?

Carolyn: Fire a parent? You mean disenroll their child?

Julie: Disenroll the child. It's a conversation that has come up before with some child care owners, about how sometimes you have parents who aren't a right match for your program. We were saying that it's like we have to fire parents.

Carolyn: Yes. We have had to disenroll families before. That's not something that I enjoy doing, but at the same time, I feel the parents need to really work with the teachers and work together. I've always been one who didn't believe—like, if you have discipline problems that come up—in shuffling a child from center to center to center. That's not fair to the child. To me, the teacher and the parent need to work together for that child. You can do that only so long, if a parent will not work with you. At that point, sometimes you just have to let the family go.

Julie: Your whole purpose in doing that is that you really focus on "It's not fair to the child."

Carolyn: Right, it's not. The child may need some outside help. It's up to us to educate the parent, to get them the resources they need. Sometimes the parent is just not willing to work with you at all. It's really hurtful for me to have to let a parent go in those circumstances, because I know it's not helping the child.

Julie: Very tough, but very important. I think that helps you maintain the vision of your whole program.

Carolyn: You also have to get rid of those parents who can't pay their bills. If you want to get new toys for your center, and your classrooms to be pretty, and pay your teachers, sometimes you have to let parents go. You hate it for the child, but it is a business as well.

Julie: That's a word that we all in this industry have to learn to embrace, that it is a business.

Carolyn: It's a business each and every day.

To hear this interview in its entirety, go to **www.ChildCareBusinessSuccess BookVault.com**. The password is **RockMyChildCare.com**.

Chapter 7

Leap Out of Overwhelm

Featuring Sindye Alexander,
Munchkin Manor Webcam Daycare

"*Whether you think you can or you can't, you're right.*"
Henry Ford

Big leaps and risks and an attitude that says "I think I can" is what make Sindye Alexander a true inspiration, and a shining example of what child care business success is all about. Just like all of the child care owners featured in this book, she is still growing and still learning. But that in and of itself is one of the true keys to success, not only in the child care industry, but also in any business model—to always be learning, always be growing.

Sindye recently posted on Facebook about a huge leap she took. She stated, "I have an absolutely amazing daycare center. In 4 short years, we have grown from 12 families in my home daycare, to 75 families, 137 children, 21 employees, and a 12,000 square foot commercial daycare building. When I looked at those numbers, I had to have a little 'party' in my office all by myself. Woo Hoo! We've come a long way, baby!! Thanks to all those who have helped me to make my dream a reality!"

It has been my pleasure to witness Sindye's journey, as we've worked closely over the past few years. She is currently in one of our mastermind programs because she is committed to her own growth personally and professionally, so that she can be the best child care owner for the community in which she serves.

One of the things that has fascinated me about Sindye is quite simply her name. It's a story that she doesn't share much, but I think is beyond powerful, as it really defines the incredible person she is. Until she was twelve years old, Sindye Alexander was known as Cindy. Same pronunciation, different spelling. But when she was twelve, she and some creative friends decided to change their names for a week or two, just to see if the teachers would notice. Sindye loved the change, and even though most of her friends changed back to the original spellings of their names, Sindye embraced the new spelling and never went back to the old.

Her name change set the tone for a life that was quite simply "not normal." But then again, whose life is normal? I love the little joke that recently circulated on social media, showing a mom and little girl. The little girl asks her mom, "What's normal, Mommy?" The mother responds, "It's just a setting on the washing machine, dear." Sindye embraces people's differences, celebrates diversity and even established the "Why Be Normal?" club in middle school. She recruited her friends to join her club, and they would get together and figure out ways to not be normal.

Sindye Alexander knows that children, in spite of their differences, should be celebrated and encouraged to bring their uniqueness to life. She has more than twenty years of hands-on experience in the child care field. She got started as a private, in-home nanny, after she married her childhood sweetheart at a young age and her first child was born. As a nanny she could take her daughter along to work. Over a period of about four years, she was a foster parent to fifteen teenage girls. She has run a family day care center licensed for six and a group day care home licensed for twelve.

When her children were grown, she thought she would get a "real" job. But she soon realized that caring for children *was* a real job and there was nothing she enjoyed doing more.

She opened Munchkin Manor Webcam Daycare in her home, complete with cameras from the start, and soon she was receiving requests to care for more children than she could accommodate. She started thinking about opening a child care center, and, after two and a half years of planning, and going back to school to earn the credits necessary to be its director, opened it in Petoskey, Michigan, in 2007.

So to what does Sindye attribute her success? Continue reading to find out.

Julie: How did you get to the point where you started your own child care program? Take us to the very beginning with you.

Sindye: Well, I was a young mom. I was fortunate enough to have met my husband in high school. I was thirteen years old on our first date. He was sixteen. We got matched up by some friends and went to a homecoming dance. Ever since that day, on October 15, 1988, we have been together. We just celebrated twenty-one years of marriage last month. We have four beautiful children. One just got married in March. She married young, like I did. When my first daughter, who will be twenty on her birthday, was born, I just didn't want to leave her. I was so excited about being a mom, and all I wanted to do was be with my baby. I didn't want to go to work and leave her to be cared for by somebody else, which is ironic, because that's what I do for a living. Not everybody has the temperament to take care of other people's kids, but I did. I was just a mom from the start. I was made to be a mom, made to be a caregiver.

Strategy 1
Treat your business as "a real job."

I started as a private nanny where I could take my daughter with me to work. From there, over the course of twenty years, life changes, things happen, husbands get new jobs and things like that. Like I said, we've done private-nanny foster care in our home, and I've run a small family center licensed for six and a group day care home licensed for twelve. I was doing that for many years when my kids were young. When all four of my children were old enough to go to school, I thought, *Great, I've done my job. They're all in school. I'm not needed at home anymore. I'll go out and get a real job.* And so I did. I went out and got my "real job." I worked at a local real estate company as a receptionist and rental agent. I liked it for about the first three or four months. It was all new and exciting. I'd never done anything like it before. But when reality set in, it did not take me long to realize that I had already been doing what I loved all those previous years—caring for kids. When I came to this conclusion, it was the happiest epiphany I had ever experienced. I love kids. And watching kids is a real job! I loved making a difference in their lives..

When I realized this, I started making plans to open Munchkin Manor. I didn't just quit my job. I made plans. I made a business plan. I had to go through the licensing process. I had to acquire equipment, and figure out a curriculum, and all those types of things. I wanted it to be a professional home day care, not just the lady in the bathrobe who's there to watch the kids. I wanted to offer preschool.

I wanted to offer learning experiences and have parents feel like they made a good child care choice. One of the things I did to help me was I installed webcams right in my home, to give parents the peace of mind that they made a good choice and could stay connected with their kids.

Julie: You had your own program out of your home when you were very young. You decided, *I'm going to have a center-based child care program.* How was that transition for you?

Sindye: It was a very exciting transition. I opened Munchkin Manor in my home in 2007. I was so excited about opening, because of my happy epiphany, like I said. I was going to be the most professional home center that I possibly could be. I was just really excited about working with kids again. Yes, I did it before, but I hadn't realized how much I loved it. When my phone kept ringing off the wall and I could not accept children anymore because my home child care was full, (I kept turning kids away), is when I started looking into opening a child care center and what it would take for me to do that. The more I looked into it, the more I thought, *This is something I can do.* It took a lot of work. I actually had to go back to school and finish some of my credits so I could be qualified to be the director of my own center. I had to look into the licensing and building codes, look at buildings, figure out how to get a loan, write a business plan, come up with funding. The more I worked at it, the more excited I got. I just felt that sense of accomplishment, just making it happen. For me it was really, really an exciting time.

Julie: You were just driven by the vision that you held tightly in yourself.

Sindye: I couldn't not be working on it. From the time that I decided I was going to open a center until it opened, it took about two and a half years of work, of planning and preparation and research, all the things that come with preparing for a center. It probably wouldn't have taken me that long if I had already had my education. I did have to finish up some of those things. I was totally driven by the vision of opening a center. I thought when I got there, I would have arrived. Little did I know that was just the beginning of everything I was going to learn.

Julie: What are the things you've learned since then? You got through all the basic education you needed, and put all the immediate tools and strategies in place. What made you say, "Wow, I need to learn this"?

Sindye: I did have some issues getting my finances in order, and moving from a small-scale home day care to a child care center. I thought it would be the same thing, just on a bigger scale. I know there are some centers mentioned in your book that have multiple locations and make millions of dollars. My center of forty kids is a huge deal for me. There's so much more involved in handling the finances of a business than just a family household. That was a learning curve for me. I've gotten a lot of help with that.

Julie: One of the things we talked about was how you, from the start, did a couple of things, even when you were doing a nanny business, to really position yourself for success. Those things had to do with the word *professionalism*.

Sindye: I'm very big on professionalism. Right from the start, even when I was doing in-home day care and working for somebody in their home, I always made sure to dress the part and conduct myself in a professional manner. I wasn't wearing business suits and stuff like that, but I would have a nice pair of khakis, or a nice pair of dark jeans, or black dress pants—none of these low-cut jeans where, when you're bending over, you-know-what is showing. That is not professional.

Julie: It does happen.

Sindye: Even if I was wearing jeans, I'd have a dress shirt on, a button-up shirt with a collar or an office-style shirt. I wanted to present myself as a professional. I wasn't just somebody babysitting. I was providing a service, and took my job seriously. When parents show up, and you're in sweatpants or the most comfortable thing you have because you know "baby Johnny is going to spit up on you anyway so why put on something nice," it doesn't send a good message. I really wanted to put forth that message about myself, that I was serious about the job I was doing. I think parents pick up on that.

Julie: So make sure you're dressing for success right from the start, even for your in-home business.

Sindye: In my home, I had an electronic time-in clock, where parents had to punch a code. Then I had the webcams in my house. I wanted them to feel there was that peace of mind that I was a quality day care and I could be trusted. They could watch what I was doing. I feel that really gives parents peace of mind. I get told over and over that even if it comes down to me and another center that somebody is considering, if there's an opening in my center, they'll take the opening here because of those webcams.

Strategy 2

Staff motivation is more than lollipops and slumber parties.

The biggest eye-opener for me was how to deal with the staff. I thought I was going to give people jobs in this wonderful new child care center, and they're professional jobs with above-average wages. We were all going to be happy to be working together, no problems, like lollipops and slumber parties all the time. That's not what happened.

We have ten different women with ten different opinions about how the room should be set up, how this kid should be cared for and disciplined, what the lesson plan and theme should be, why this staff person does such and such this way. There were all these little fires to put out that, to the staff, seemed pretty significant. I felt like it was just minute stuff. *Why couldn't they just get along? Why does everything have to be such a big deal?* It took me some time to figure out how to professionally address issues with staff, where to draw boundaries and how to let them know what I expect from them, while still giving them the freedom to make their own choices in how they go about stuff. Staff issues were my biggest eye-opener. I felt I was floundering, until I found your Dream Team Bootcamp. That helped me so much.

Julie: That's so fantastic to hear, that the Dream Team Bootcamp really got you on the straight and narrow with your staff. We find this a lot. Having your staff function as a dynamic, happy team automatically is a myth of being in business. It's like, *Here's this vision, and now we should all be happy and work together.* Then we find out it doesn't work that way. We've gotten calls from people who've been in the business five years, fifteen years, thirty years, and they're still struggling with staff motivation issues.

Sindye: I have twenty years of experience in child care, but I have only three years of experience running a center. When I was doing child care, it was me, myself and I, or it was me and my husband, or me and one assistant. It was me and one other person, at the most. Now that I'm in a center, there are probably ten or eleven teachers here right now in the building. They all have their assignments. We run as a cohesive team now. Everybody is pitching in to help each other. If one of my staff has a family emergency, everybody else pitches in to cover the shift. I have a really great team now. That first year, boy, did I go through some people. I needed you so badly.

Julie: I'm glad I was able to help. Now your experiences just make you wiser in your position. I'm sure that's helping you to say, "I really have a lot to offer other child care owners who are going to be launching in the same direction as me." You have a bigger vision now, and that's to actually get in there and help other child care owners with their programs, right?

Sindye: Yeah. I just have a strong heart and a strong vision to help empower other child care business owners with a lot of things that I've learned the hard way.

Julie: When it comes to staff motivation, let's say we're going to start the process of hiring staff or getting our ideal team members in place. What is it you would recommend to people?

Sindye: I would say have a clear idea of what you're looking for before you start hiring. I've had it happen a few times, and I've made the mistake, where somebody walked through the door with a résumé, and I sort of do need someone, and this person seems willing, and they seem nice, so I'll give them a try. I didn't really do my research. I definitely need to know what the qualifications are. Assistants and lead teachers don't always need the same qualifications. Then you need to know you're asking the right questions, and that you have well-thought-out interview questions. You definitely need to take the time to ask for references and to make those phone calls. I have been guilty of not calling, because I felt like I had a really good idea of what this person was like because they presented well at the interview. You don't know how many times somebody is presentable at the interview but after the fact weren't so good, or that I learned if I had only called and checked that reference, I might have made a different decision. At the same time, there is an element of trusting your gut. You know if somebody is going to be a fit, or could be a fit, based on a couple initial interactions with that person.

Julie: I like what you're saying, to really have an idea in your mind of what this person looks like and what they're all about.

Sindye: Yes, ahead of time. Don't just pick anybody.

Strategy 3
Marketing starts with a professional website.

Julie: If someone were to come to you and ask, "Sindye, what is the most powerful marketing strategy that you've implemented that's also sure to inspire people to come through my doors?," what would that be?

Sindye: I think having a professional website that includes an opt-in box, where parents can opt in to get more information, whether you're offering a free report on potty training or a quiz to see whether or not your child is meeting their milestones. So offer some sort of free expert guide or report on your website. Then have them sign up to get your newsletters or other free gifts and information. Having those autoresponders set up is really key in staying in front of your prospects. Maybe some of the older generations still use the Yellow Pages. But today's generation, myself included, if I want to know some information or look up a phone number, I just type on my smartphone or computer to look up a plumber, a day care, a pizza place. You type it in, and that's where you get the information and the phone number.

If you don't have a quality website, one that doesn't look like some hodgepodge thing your thirteen-year-old daughter put together for you, you're losing people right there. People absolutely have to be able to find you on the Internet. Then once they find you, you need to give them a reason to stay in contact with you. Every once in a while, you need to be throwing them a bone, an e-mail. It doesn't always have to be, "Come to our day care center because we're the best in town." It can just be, "We thought you might like these potty-training tips. Did you know the state police is offering free carseat safety next Saturday at two o'clock?" It can be friendly, something to put you out there as an expert, helpful. Even if they were just browsing your website right now, looking at something for the future, you should be the first place they think of when they're ready.

I've developed a series of e-mails and autoresponders that are graphically appealing. They cover all different types of subjects that parents would be interested in. As a busy daycare director and owner, it is almost impossible to find the time to put together visually appealing e-mails with great HTML design, graphics or photos, and stuff like that, let alone to come up with the ideas and content for these e-mails. So I've made the process easy for owners.

Julie: If the Internet did not exist, what would you say is your best marketing strategy? I know chances are very slim that the Internet would disappear, but one of the ways I always think about my business is, *If I didn't have this tool, what would I have to do to still get clients, to still get customers?* If the Internet went away, and you had to rely on other types of marketing, more brick-and-mortar, traditional marketing, which you probably still use right now, what would you say is one of your biggest success secrets when it comes to that?

Sindye: I would say have a system for follow-up, even if it's not an autoresponder. I also set a timer to remind myself to call clients after their first thirty days. I send them a card after they've enrolled. They want to feel like they matter to you. We are taking care of the most precious thing in their lives, their children. If they feel like your business is a machine without real love, there will be a disconnect. Now of course, behind the scenes you want your business to operate like a machine, but if parents feel like they're dropping off their child and a machine is watching their baby and just keeping it safe, and that you're pressing buttons to feed and diaper the child, they won't be happy. Parents are more than willing to go somewhere else that will either offer them a better price or another bell and whistle. They need to feel like you're emotionally invested in them. Show them that you really care about what happens to their family, and you care if they're going through a tough time or you celebrate their child's graduation to the next classroom. They might have older kids with a high school graduation or something. Keep in touch with them. Just know what's going on in their lives, and make comments. Know their family, know their child and care about them. I think that is one of the key things with client retention.

Julie: That's very powerful. Knowing that you care increases their confidence in your service and this goes a long way.

Sindye: So just a personal note, conversations at pick-up and drop-off, and maybe some personal cards, a phone call.

Julie: When you transitioned into having a commercial, center-based child care, what do you think was one of the most critical steps you took to get people through your door? Was it advertising in the newspaper? Was it going out there and preaching your message and what you were about and how you're here to serve?

Sindye: I did several things. I did some e-mail marketing, and some flyer marketing. I mailed flyers, and a little letter to pediatricians' offices, the hospital, OB/GYN offices, teachers at every elementary school in the county. "My day care is open evening and weekend hours." I also e-mailed and/or mailed flyers to several restaurants, hotels and factories, where I knew parents worked odd shifts and may need care during nonstandard hours. And then, as we started getting closer to opening the new center, I kept information on every single phone call that I received. I made sure to stay in contact with these leads and let them know, "Hey, it looks like our new center is going to be opening in February. We're going to be having an open house, and we'd love for you to come." I'd just stay in contact with those leads who seemed really interested in enrolling their children, kept them updated. I had a great open house. We opened up the new center full.

Strategy 4

Create systems.

Julie: Opened the new center full, that's pretty good. Was there anything else, besides motivating the staff, that you had to become an expert on? Was there anything else that really made you think, *Wow, here's another change we need to make to keep the enthusiasm going?*

Sindye: Yes. That is the creation of systems and processes. I had my own way of doing things when I was the cook and the bookkeeper and the invoicing lady and the diaper changer and the preschool planner and everything in my home day care.

Julie: You're making my head spin.

Sindye: I think child care business owners and directors are like superheroes. They have to be able to put on that cape and put out fires, save the day, whether it's clearing a clogged toilet, filling in inside a classroom, getting that paperwork done on time or finding a solution to whatever problem there is. You have to be able to wear so many hats, keep so many balls juggling in the air. I have learned how to create systems. I've learned how to deal with staff.

I've experienced a lot of roadblocks and pitfalls that I'm sure many other child care business owners and directors are experiencing or have experienced. Any home day care provider knows exactly what I'm talking about. When I transitioned to a commercial center and had staff that were doing all these things, not everybody did everything the same way. What was working for me didn't necessarily get communicated to other people. Then one person would empty the garbage and not put extra bags at the bottom of the bin, which would upset somebody else who likes to empty the garbage and have an extra bag in the bin so they don't need to go look for the box of garbage bags. For even minute things like that, you must have an operation system. It's a work in progress that we're always perfecting. We created an operations manual. Let's say Sally, who normally does invoicing, is out for the week, and I need someone else to step in to do it. There's a list of instructions with everything that needs to be done.

Julie: That's fantastic. Let's break down what systems actually are. You think systems are a big thing. Really, you can have systems in place for just about everything, even for how you turn on the lights in the morning or close the doors at night.

Sindye: You can have systems in place for how you brush your teeth. It is so simple. I felt so overwhelmed in the beginning, like, *Oh, my God, there's so much to figure out, and do, and communicate.* When you put systems in place, basically what that means is you decide, *This is how we're going to do this particular thing*, even if it's, *We're putting the toilet paper roll with the paper on the upside.* We decide this is how we're going to do this particular thing. We put it in writing. That way, when somebody has a question, or you have new staff coming in and they're not really sure how to do something, or maybe it's something one particular staff member does all the time and they never have to consult the book but another staff member has to step up and help in this particular area, they can consult the book and know exactly what to do. It's basically just instructions, or an agreed-upon way of completing a task.

Julie: We've been teaching about systems for a long time. They really are key for helping business owners get more freedom and have more time. That's one asset that business owners don't get enough of, time. This is a critically important lesson. If you get anything from this interview with Sindye, get this part, that systems are so incredibly important.

Are you willing to share any of your systems with us?

Sindye: Some of the systems have to do with operations. That's really after you come up with systems for these other areas. It all falls together to create that operations manual. Some of the systems I like to talk about are systems for hiring. You need to know: How are you going to keep your paperwork? What questions are you going to ask at the interview? Do you have a standard policy to have a second interview? Are you ever going to hire right on the spot? What is your system for checking and keeping records, of checking references, things like that?

You need to have systems for all of your record-keeping that's involved with a child care center. Any director knows that every state requires you to keep certain things in a child's file. Some of those things have to be updated annually. When you get a new enrollment, what is your system? How is that entered into your child care software or management system? A lot of people use something like EZ-Care2 or those types of programs. How is that going to be entered? Are you keeping only paper copies, or are you scanning those and keeping digital copies as well? How are you going to remind yourself when the next health appraisal is going to be due? How are you going to remind the parents when that needs to be done? You need record-keeping systems.

You need systems for training new employees, and that goes for hiring too. I'm just going off the top of my head. When you hire a new employee, there are certain things they have to be trained in.

You have to make sure you get their shaken baby syndrome and sudden infant death syndrome training hours in there. You have to make sure that bloodborne pathogens training is done. You have to make sure they have their CPR card and that you run their criminal background check. Then the training of that staff member as well. There are certain things you have to make sure are covered. Your operations manual will certainly help you out with that.

You need systems for talking with the parents, like your daily reports. A system for whether or not you want the lead teacher to always be the one talking with the parents, or if the assistant caregivers are welcome to do that as well. And I guess some communication guidelines. I never want my staff to lie or keep something from a parent, but I always want it portrayed in the best light. If little Johnny was a devil today, I'm not saying, "He bit three kids, and he was jumping off the chair, and I couldn't keep him still." Mom is not going to appreciate the fact that it seems to her like her child is a burden to us. You might say something like, "Johnny was really active today, a little bit of a rough patch, but we turned it around by the end of the day." I don't want to keep anything from parents. Sometimes, if a really concerning issue comes up, we have to have a parent-teacher conference about it. There are guidelines you might want to make sure your staff know when communicating with parents.

Julie: These are really critical. Think about all the mental energy that is consumed when you don't have a system in place. Then it's, *Oh, this happened, but what do we do now?* A parent leaves a center. What do we do now? A staff member leaves the center. Who do we communicate with? How do we do that? So many different things come up that drain your time and suck away your energy. Having these systems in place really gives you back that time, helps remotivate you and helps you have more energy.

Sindye: One of the ways I realized I needed to create systems is that staff would keep asking me the same questions over and over.

Julie: That's a big sign.

Sindye: They'd say, "I want to take a vacation day for such and such day that I was sick." I'd write it on a sticky note, and then I'd have to remember on the payroll day to document it. Now we have a system for how they can let us know when they want to use vacation days. Nobody has to exchange words at all. It's entered in there, and we know what to check, and it's done.

Strategy 5

Find your uniqueness.

Julie: One thing that inquiring minds want to know is, "How did you come up with your child care program name, Munchkin Manor?"

Sindye: I used Thesaurus.com. I was looking for different names. I wanted it to be something catchy that was either an alliteration or a rhyme. A friend of mine takes her daughter to a day care in a town far away from me. The name was Sugar and Spice Daycare. I wanted something like that, something you could remember. I was looking for synonyms for children, for house, for care and all that. I landed on Munchkin Manor. I thought it was such a catchy and original name. Then I looked it up on the Internet after I'd already decided on it, and there were a bunch of Munchkin Manors out there. I'm the only Munchkin Manor Webcam Daycare.

Julie: Isn't it funny how we search and search for original ideas, and then there they are, all over the place?

Sindye: Somebody had already thought of it, but I came up with it on my own without realizing there were other Munchkin Manors. I decided to keep it because I liked it.

Julie: You also have a very interesting story to tell us about your name. You are a unique person who is filled with enthusiasm. One of the ways people can remember you is definitely by the uniqueness of your name. Share with us that quick story on how we often confuse your name.

Sindye: My name is Sindye Alexander. It sounds like the regular "Cindy," but I spell it like a freakazoid. I spell my name S-I-N-D-Y-E. Why did I do that? When I was twelve years old, I was looking to be different and creative. Some of my friends and I decided we were going to change our names in school for a week or two, just to see if the teachers noticed. This is the spelling I came up with then. It just stuck. I loved it. My friend Angie changed her name to A-H-N-J-I. I wish she would have kept that, because I thought that was so cool. I kept Sindye. It is just regular "Cindy," but with an S and a silent E at the end. My mother did not like it. She still calls me Cynthia. She says, "I named you Cynthia for a reason. It was the most beautiful name I could think of." She still calls me Cynthia, and so do all of my aunts and uncles, but my friends call me Sindye. People get confused all the time and call me Sidney. I understand. I'm not making it easy for them. If you look at my name real quick, it does look like Sidney, but it's Sindye.

Julie: It makes you unique.

Sindye: Speaking of unique, about the same period of my life, when I was in middle school, I started the "Why Be Normal?" club. I actually had people who would come to this club after school, and we'd figure out how to not be normal.

Julie: Always searching for your uniqueness. That's very interesting. That's a good story to tell.

Sindye: It's a silly story.

Julie: It's about who you are. I think in marketing, part of driving people to your website is to share a little bit of a personal story about yourself. I think this would be a cool one to put out there, to say, "We help kids find their uniqueness, because I myself wanted to be unique from the time I was such-and-such years old." That's a great marketing strategy right there, to tap into your uniqueness for your website and for your own marketing materials. Tell a story with it. To me, telling the story, even about your name or the "Why Be Normal?" club, that is a cool thing to share with parents.

Sindye: I do have a story on the website, but it's more professional. It doesn't have that silly tidbit about my twelve-year-old self on there.

Julie: Parents may come to you saying, "My kid's not normal." You'll understand, because, of course, you founded the "Why Be Normal?" club.

Sindye: Along with that, I do things differently at my day care than a lot of traditional centers do—with the webcams, with the parents who work nights, with the extended hours, and things like that. We are stepping outside the box somewhat in the day care center as well.

Julie: During these Child Care Business Success interviews, own-ers have revealed their original ideas for their programs, as well as their stories about how they came to be who they are. When you go to their websites, those stories are missing. People want to hear the stories in order to connect with you, especially when you're an owner in a center and you're active there. That story is a reflection of that business and who you are. Let me know how it goes.

Sindye: I might add the tidbit about that. Thank you.

Julie: Sometimes we have to search for those things. You're lucky you don't have to search too far. I really encourage everybody to think about why you do what you do, and get in touch with that.

Then that's something you can share with the child care world or with parents who are searching for quality child care.

Strategy 6
Have faith.

Sindye: One thing I want to mention, as far as growing from a home center into a child care center, or any growth that you're experiencing, whether you're adding to your capacity or changing a program, is adding another location. Roadblocks are going to pop up along the way. I remember a roadblock I had when I was first opening this center. I staked my life on the line. I mortgaged my house to be able to get a small business loan. I put in every cent of my personal savings, and tax refunds, and everything else, to be able to get the business up and off the ground. We had to do some remodeling right before we opened, to bring the building up to code. There was a fee that the building department wanted us to pay. It was a ridiculous fee, the paperwork fee. It was $6,000, because we changed the zoning of our building from business to educational. That was almost crippling, devastating. I didn't know if I was going to be able to even open the doors after that. I'd had everything planned out to the penny of what I needed. There also have been other roadblocks along the way.

There are things you find out, either a financial roadblock, or that somebody isn't happy with your program, or that a staff member is causing problems for you. You just think, *What else is going to happen? I might as well throw in the towel.* I would just like to encourage everybody to persevere. I've got a quote on my wall. It says, "Failure plus perseverance equals success." There's another quote I love. "Whether you think you can or you can't, you're right." It all comes down to your mindset, what you're willing to do. Once you make that commitment to press on, things just fall out of the sky to make it all happen for you. You cannot see in your own little human mind how you're going to get through this next step. You just decide you're going to keep going and keep doing what it takes. Once you make that commitment, it happens. I just want to encourage people to not lose hope if they're feeling like, *I don't know what I'm going to do next. I don't know what I can do differently to make my situation better.* It can be done. Keep the faith.

Julie: Keep the faith. Open yourself up to the possibilities of what you can do. That's very powerful. It's true, we all have different paths for growing our businesses. We get to a certain level, and it's like, *Wait a second, I'm not comfortable with this. Now I'm going to have to invest more money. This isn't going to work.* Just keep opening yourself up to the possibilities—I love that.

Strategy 7
Position yourself as "the expert."

Julie: Is there anything you would like to add in closing?

Sindye: Well, I'm just really excited to be a part of this book. When you introduced me earlier, at the beginning of the interview, you called me a child care business expert. I actually chuckled to myself a little bit, because it sounds funny to hear somebody else describe me that way. But the more I think about it, I am. I have twenty years of experience. I have run the gamut of every child care situation. I have found a way to make the business successful and make it fun. I love my job. I love what I do. I thought when I started on this journey, that when I opened my center I would have arrived. I realize that I have just begun what I want to do.

Julie: That's very powerful. Once you thought you got there, it really just began. A lot of people who study success think it's a fallacy to assume it's a destination. Success is a continuous journey that we engage upon. With each new venture, you're going to end up in a different place. Then be ready for a new journey along that path.

Sindye: It definitely is a journey. Like I said, I thought once I opened the center, that would be it. It's not. I had to learn so much about operating the center. I have done that successfully, and now I'm starting to share that with other child care business owners. The reason is because I want to help people, whether it be kids or other people who want to help kids. I want to help people.

To hear this interview in its entirety, go to **www.ChildCareBusinessSuccess BookVault.com**. The password is **RockMyChildCare.com**.

Chapter 8

Building Your Reputation as "The Best"

Featuring Phyllis Regan, The Carousel School

"Every successful individual knows that his or her achievement depends on a community of persons working together."

Paul Ryan

First clients . . . Do you remember yours? I remember all of mine. They hold a special place in my heart. I think about how they found me, how I helped them, their stories, their staff and of course, their passion for what they do. I never seem to forget the passion I feel when I'm in a child care owner's presence.

One of my first clients was a woman by the name of Phyllis Regan. Phyllis approached me about doing a team-building day for her staff at her school in Waltham, Massachusetts. When I first began my business, I marketed myself by using many of Dan Kennedy's strategies. If you don't know who Dan is, he's the go-to source for direct mail marketing that converts prospects into customers or clients. It's really great stuff. Back to Phyllis. She discovered a flyer in her mailbox that I sent to her. She felt pulled in and reached out to me.

When I conducted my initial consultation with Phyllis, I found out that she already had a fantastic team. So I asked her, "What are you hoping to accomplish through a program with me?" She said, "It's simple. I want to keep my team strong and take communication to a whole new level." Well, we had a great team-building program, and now, for sixteen years in a row, her center has been voted the best preschool in Waltham, Massachusetts! So of course, this wonderful woman holds a special place in my heart. I couldn't put this first book out there without sharing with you her story.

So where did the journey start for one of my first clients? Phyllis became the director of The Carousel School in Waltham by accident. Literally.

Hop in the time machine with me back to 1962. One of the Number One songs was "I Can't Stop Loving You" by Ray Charles, and the president of the United States was John F. Kennedy. Speaking of love, Phyllis's husband is the main culprit in this story, as to how Phyllis ended up owning a preschool program.

He had bought some property, and, wouldn't you know it, the property had a nursery school already on it. He thought that maybe his parents would be interested in running the nursery school. But that was a someday thought. He knew that in the meantime the school was his to run. And then life changes in a minute . . .

One March morning, a car hit the school's Volkswagen bus in an intersection near the school. What's a wife to do when her husband calls and says, "Phyllis, I need you." She was at home with their two youngest children, a two-and-a-half-year-old and an eight-month-old. Their oldest was in kindergarten. But when her husband called, she dropped her plans, packed up the children and took them with her to help her husband manage the chaos at the preschool. In a minute, this stay-at-home mom transitioned gracefully to the director and owner of a preschool.

Just as I remember Phyllis, one of my first clients, Phyllis has a special place in her heart for her very first preschool class. On March 14 her very first activity with the children was making shamrocks. She's been having fun at the school ever since. She later had a fourth child, who also went to Carousel, as did her grandchildren and a great-granddaughter. She believes that understanding child development made her a better mother.

I asked Phyllis to share the philosophies and practices that help make the Waltham center stand above the rest. How does it feel being voted "the best" for the very first time, let alone sixteen years in a row? Let's tune in to my conversation with Phyllis and discover her response.

Phyllis: We were just so happy. I had one teacher, who is now not with us. She passed away from cancer five years ago. But every year in August, since the first time we won the award, she'd always call me and say, "Phyllis, have you heard? Have you heard?" Of course, we didn't hear until almost Labor Day. She was so excited for us. I still think of her when we get the vote. She worked with me for twenty-eight years. Her husband came just yesterday and helped us with our computers. He's still helping us.

Julie: Tell us a little bit about your program. What size are you guys? How many kids, how many staff?

Phyllis: We're licensed for sixty-two children. Most of our children come either from nine o'clock to eleven forty-five or nine o'clock to one o'clock, two, three or five days a week. Our staff, we have fourteen teachers plus the administrators that work with me every day.

Julie: Fantastic. Phyllis, how did you get started?

Phyllis: How did I get started? This is almost a fairy tale. My husband called me one day in 1962. I had an eight-month-old, a two-and-a-half-year-old and a five-year-old. My husband said he needed me. There was a school bus accident in front of the school. At that time, he was running the school. I already had a business degree. From that time on, I just went down and continued my education to get my degree in early childhood special needs. I've been working ever since. It's been a wonderful, wonderful journey, and I've enjoyed every single day of it. My oldest child was going to kindergarten, but my second child, David, and my third child, Kim, came to school with me. Then I had a fourth child, Timothy, and they all went to Carousel. I've also had my grandchildren come to Carousel. My great-granddaughter, Isabelle, just graduated last year after spending three years with me. We've seen generations of families go through Carousel.

Julie: I have to back up a little bit more. When this accident happened, how did you make the transition from this thing happening and—Was it a school where he was working?

Phyllis: It was in the intersection by the nursery school. A car hit the bus. At that time they had a Volkswagen school bus. He called to say he needed me to come down there and help him. I went down. It was March 14, right before St. Patrick's Day. I can remember the first lesson I did with the children. We made shamrocks. Those are some of the things that stay with you. From that day on, I just stayed to help him at the school.

Julie: So you stayed there and helped him work at the school. How do you go from helping your husband work at a school because there was an accident, to now being the owner of this child care program?

Phyllis: My husband had bought the piece of property, and the school was on the property. My husband was the owner of the land. He thought at that time his mother and father might be interested in running the school. In those days, a lot of the schools weren't licensed as they are now. The person who owned it before had been a registered nurse, and her husband had owned it before that.

Julie: So your husband owned the property the school was on. Then there was the accident, and you stepped in and just never left. Now you own and run the program.

Phyllis: Um-hmm.

Julie: So it was a natural slide in there for you.

Phyllis: It just happened. I always thought when my children were young I'd be a police lady or a foster care mother. Instead I became a teacher and director at a preschool.

Julie: That's really cool. Looking back at your entire journey, what do you think is one of the best lessons that you've learned from owning a child care program?

Strategy 1

Keep learning.

Phyllis: Continuing my education. I think by continuing going to school and taking courses and staying abreast of early childhood education, it's made me a better mother, understanding child development. The people I've met in the courses I've taken, and being involved with both the NAEYC (National Association for the Education of Young Children) and its Boston affiliate, and the National Association of Child Care, I just think staying involved has kept me and my staff abreast of all that's happening in early childhood. It's kept me aware of the changes in licensing too. Massachusetts has strict licensing. I was also a validator for NAEYC. That was quite an experience, going around Massachusetts and validating programs. That was a whole new experience for me.

Julie: I can imagine. One of the biggest challenges, a lot of times, is what child care owners and child care directors face with their staff. Tell me about your staff, and your retention statistics, and all that good stuff.

Strategy 2

Hire staff who support your philosophy.

Phyllis: The staff person who's with me right now, Mrs. Pam, she called me when she just graduated from college. She was looking for a position. At that time I did not have an opening, but I hired her as a floater. She's now going on her thirty-fourth year with me, and she's my right-hand administrative assistant. I just think I hired people who really brought our philosophy to Carousel. I have my two sisters-in-law, my two brothers' wives, working with me also. Linda just celebrated her thirtieth year here at Carousel. Ginger is going on her eighteenth year at Carousel. In addition to having parents I know who have substituted at Carousel, and all have their degrees, their children came to Carousel, and they now work at Carousel. I always have a waiting list of parents for substitute teachers. I can handpick my staff. That's really made a very caring community of teachers who all respect each other.

Julie: What were you saying earlier, 90 percent of your staff?

Phyllis: Ninety percent of my staff were parents first. My two sisters-in-law's children had come to Carousel first. Only two staff people, one didn't have any children and the other's children were older. I was able to get her through my best friend. I needed a teacher, and it was her sister-in-law's sister. She's going on twenty-nine years with me.

Julie: That's amazing. How do you think your program differs from the others in your area, since you guys were voted the best? Were there comments that you got to read where you can figure out why people like you better?

Strategy 3

Help parents feel the difference.

Phyllis: I think when parents come to visit, when they do the tour of the program and see our facilities and meet our staff, see our children all happy, and we have visitors who come in and do different enrichment programs at our school—I think it's a feeling that you get when you walk into the program. You just know that the children are really being taken care of, and that the teachers are attentive to each child. I think the parents feel the same way when they're arriving in the morning or in the afternoon to pick up their child. I think this is an instinct you get. You can feel the love for every child and every family. I just met two parents who are sisters. Their children are all in college, and one of them is getting married. They were just saying it all began at Carousel. It's so wonderful to read in the newspapers about our children, how they're doing well in sports and colleges and plays. It's a great feeling, seeing the success and hearing the stories all the time, whether I'm in the supermarket or at the Cape, hearing the wonderful parents commenting. One of the teachers from my school, who my granddaughter just finished kindergarten with, is now a teacher at Northeast Elementary School. He's got the best reputation at the school. He just taught one of my teacher's children this past school year. It's wonderful keeping in touch with him and hearing his success stories also.

Julie: That's fantastic. You say when you're out there, whether it's at the grocery store or the Cape, you hear things from parents. What sort of things do you hear?

Phyllis: How wonderfully their children are doing, and they all attribute it to the beginning the children got. It all began at Carousel.

Julie: You hear that over and over and over again.

Phyllis: I was at a birthday party for one of my friends. Her grandson had just completed his first year of college at Notre Dame. Just talking to him and listening to him explain . . . They talk about times when we did the pony rides at the end of the school year, the fun times they can remember. A lot of these children have become such good friends. My youngest son, Timothy, and his best friend, Jerry, were in each other's weddings. They've made lifelong friendships. And parents say the same thing. They're always telling me they've met so many friends at Carousel. It's an ongoing caring for each other.

Julie: That's fantastic. When it comes to marketing strategies, is there anything else, besides all this fantastic word of mouth that's out there about you and your program, that you put into practice every year to keep your marketing alive and to keep your waiting list growing?

Strategy 4
Always ask: How did you hear about us?

Phyllis: We send a picture of The Carousel School on a postcard to all the new homeowners. When people come to the school, we ask who recommended Carousel or how they heard about us. People say they got the postcard. They didn't even have any children when they got the postcard, but they remember when it's time to send their children to Carousel. That's one of the memories they have, of receiving the postcard in the mail. I feel as though that's been one of my unique marketing procedures that has brought children to Carousel.

Julie: So a welcoming postcard to all new families. Does your postcard just say, "Welcome to the neighborhood," or do you do anything special with it?

Phyllis: It says, "Welcome to Waltham," and we describe our program. We say, "If you'd like to visit, give us a call." Right now we have a really good website. We get most of our referrals from our website. People just see the website and call. That seems to bring in a lot of new families.

Julie: What is your website, Phyllis?

Phyllis: Carouselschool.org.

Julie: Is there anything else you do with marketing, or do you figure postcard and website, you're good?

Phyllis: We do newsletters. We have online newsletters. Those go out to the parents. We have them online for the parent-access part of our website. The parents can then send their families pictures of their children that run in the newsletters. I think that really helps with the marketing.

Julie: That's a constant touchpoint for the parents to have with you.

Phyllis: We still advertise in church bulletins, and that also brings new families to the school.

Julie: So advertising, church bulletins, welcoming postcards. Is there one that you feel is the most successful?

Strategy 5

Survey parents.

Phyllis: I think the marketing is the families. Once a year we do a parent survey. We have parents give permission for us to give out their phone numbers on a list. New prospective parents can then call parents on that list. I think that has really been a positive way of getting families. They like to talk to another family that has attended Carousel.

Julie: That's true. So basically when you have parents who come in and tour, you provide them with a piece of paper with the phone numbers of parents who say they can call as a reference?

Phyllis: They gave us permission to use their phone numbers, right. That's one of the questions on our survey that we do once a year.

Julie: That's really good. So you ask your current parents once a year if it's okay to include them on that list?

Phyllis: Um-hmm.

Julie: That's fantastic. What else is on that survey? Is it all about satisfaction and that sort of thing?

Phyllis: Yes. The national association has a survey, and we made our own survey. It's after suggestions and comments. One of the parents had said that it was difficult, especially in the wintertime, to get here because we're on a private street in a private location. What we've done now is, we have the upstairs children, the younger children, come from nine o'clock to eleven forty-five, and the downstairs children, the older children, they come from eight forty-five to eleven thirty or twelve forty-five, making the road easier to drop off and pick up children. That was just one comment. This mother who had suggested that had been a student at Carousel, and her third child is going to be coming in September.

Julie: So you are really a preschool, as opposed to a child care center, right?

Phyllis: Yes, we are a preschool. We're open from seven thirty to four o'clock, but most of our children come part time, either two, three or five days. We do have some children who arrive between seven thirty and eight forty-five. Most of those are teachers' children. Most of them are part time, because a lot of our families do have family members who take care of the children on the days they don't attend Carousel. We used to be a day care, and we'd be open from six o'clock in the morning to six o'clock at night. Now, like I said, it's seven thirty to four o'clock. Those are the hours that our parents need.

Julie: You probably found that out through the surveys, right?

Phyllis: Yes. We're open from September to June. We're not open summers anymore.

Julie: You've got a nice little break.

Phyllis: Right. We do administration and maintenance during the summer.

Julie: What does your daily routine look like, Phyllis, on a typical day?

Phyllis: For myself?

Julie: For yourself, for running your program. Inquiring minds want to know.

Phyllis: I'm up every morning at five o'clock. I'm usually at the school at eight o'clock. I have assistants who help me with the program, with the parents. It's greeting the children, meeting with the staff, attending meetings. It's a pretty busy day. I probably go to bed by nine o'clock at night.

Julie: Is there a structured routine that you have while you're at the school?

Strategy 6
Keep your curriculum fun for you.

Phyllis: It's visiting the classrooms, doing observations, meeting with the parents, referring children. We refer children for occupational therapy, physical therapy, speech or eyeglasses. We work with different local school departments. We have people coming in and observing with the children, and meeting with the parents, to provide the services. We work with Enable, which was founded by the Department of Education. Its liaison has been wonderful the last five years, coming and helping children if they have any behavioral issues, or any issues going on in the family, that they need help with. It's a very busy day. We don't take the children on field trips, but we have people come in to do plays. We had a wonderful person, Kyle Die, come this year to do one on allergies that was fantastic. We work with Tufts University. They come and do plays both in the spring and the fall. We have the New England Aquarium come and bring all the different starfish and things so the children can do hands-on activities. Instead of taking the children to the aquarium, they come to us. We have puppet shows, music, a sports program that comes. Stacy Tully comes and does music and movement dance. Scheduling all these different enrichment programs is busy. It's very, very busy maintaining the curriculum. Like I said, we have the pony rides, and they bring goats, ducks, chickens and lambs to school in June, so the children have a petting zoo besides having pony rides. We have the firemen come. We have a lot of firemen's children at Carousel, so they bring the firetruck right into the driveway and let the children get on the firetruck and squirt the hose and put on the hats and shoes. We have police officers come for Halloween and do a safety program. A woman police officer tells all the children about how to be safe for Halloween. We have Santa Claus and the Easter Bunny. We do all the holidays. It's a pretty full school year. We have a lot of things planned.

Julie: It sounds like there's a lot going on at The Carousel School.

Phyllis: We have fun every day.

Julie: What are your tips for planning curriculum? With all that going on, are there any tips you would say help you stay organized with this?

Phyllis: We do the Handwriting Without Tears program. That's been quite successful with the children and the staff. That's done with music also. The staff is really energized about doing that program.

Julie: What about from an owner's or director's perspective, thinking, *How do I plan all this curriculum?* Are there any strategies that you plan or implement to make sure your curriculum is a successful one?

Phyllis: We have monthly teachers' meetings. I meet with teachers often, as far as listening to them and having them also contribute. Some teachers are really good in science. Some teachers are really good in literacy. They've shared with me as far as developing the curriculum. We've checked with the different schools, because we probably serve maybe six to eight communities, to find out if the children who are graduating from our program are meeting the benchmarks for the schools they're going into. They all say they can tell the children from Carousel are ready for kindergarten because of the training they've had at Carousel.

Julie: Fantastic. That must give you the warm fuzzies inside.

Phyllis: It's wonderful to know that the kindergarten teachers enjoy having our students enrolled in their classes.

Julie: With your curriculum, is it just a matter of you sitting down, planning it out, writing it down on a piece of paper and it all comes together?

Phyllis: The teachers do that.

Julie: So how far in advance are you planning?

Phyllis: They plan for the whole school year. They do it month by month, but they plan out so the children are actually doing different things different months. They do the seasons. This year they did a lot on manners, because some of the children were having difficulty. What they do is they send out suggestions to the parents by e-mail, so the parents can be working on what the children are working on at school, working together with the families. Right now, when parents enroll their children, it's not just the child who's enrolled in

178

the preschool. It's the whole family that we enroll, because we work together with the family so the child really has a positive preschool experience.

Julie: That's a fantastic way of looking at it. Phyllis, if you were speaking to a group of preschool owners or child care owners, what are the three biggest success tips you would give to them?

Strategy 7
Build a community.

Phyllis: I think the most important is your staff. I think the staff, along with the parents, provide the education for the children. I think everyone has to respect each other and contribute, so that the whole building has that feeling, when you go to enroll your child, that this is where I'd like to be. This is what the parents say to us when they come. The parents do come in and volunteer and read stories. They help out. They're always amazed at how well the children are listening, following directions. I think a lot of it is the staff. As far as the community, I think it's giving back to the community also. I think you have to be available in different organizations, so that they know you're there. Really loving what you do every day is important, to share that enthusiasm and encouragement and to be there for the families and staff.

Julie: Your staff, loving what you do and being out in the community are three of the biggest success tips?

Phyllis: I think so. I think the community is important.

Julie: Is there anything special that you do with the community, or is it just a matter of joining different organizations?

Phyllis: Right. I've been very active in the city of Waltham. I was named woman of the year by the women's association. I've been very active in the Waltham Jaycees. My husband is very active in politics. We're always part of the community.

Julie: So people always know you.

Phyllis: People always know me, yes.

Julie: What are the things that you would tell leaders, directors and owners out there? What things should you probably not do if you want to be successful in running a child care program?

Phyllis: I think confidentiality is one of the most important things, and impress that on your staff too. Teachers cannot go out and talk about the children in the community. I think we really have to respect the families.

Julie: That would be the biggest thing?

Phyllis: I think you really have to be aware of each family and respect them.

Julie: What is the biggest challenge that you overcame to be successful with what you're doing?

Phyllis: I think the biggest challenge is to continue to stay fully enrolled, so that you can continue to provide jobs for the employees you have. Like you were saying, marketing—make the most of it so your school can be successful.

Julie: Was there ever a time when your enrollment dropped and you were like, *Oh, my goodness, how are we going to get more kids in here?*

Phyllis: There were times when the economy was down, but I was able to continue to keep my staff and not lay anyone off. I think I showed my staff that I invested a lot into them and it was important to do.

Julie: How did you get enrollment back up?

Strategy 8

When enrollment is low, get your name out there—everywhere.

Phyllis: We put up posters in the library. We'd have pajama parties at the library, and have our children come there. We put little articles in the newspapers of all the events, having Santa Claus come or giving special awards. I think this was a way of just keeping our name out there, so that they knew we were still in our location.

Julie: Posters in the library, continuous press releases being written about things going on, those are good ideas.

Phyllis: And posters in the supermarkets, posters at the dental offices and pediatricians' offices, sending out letters to the pediatricians in our community. This is probably one of the things I forgot to say to you. I think the biggest thing is to send thank-you notes to the parents when they recommend the school, to the pediatricians when they recommend us, to anyone else. You can never say "thank you" enough to people for helping you out.

Julie: That's true. We even find that with staff motivation, during my programs. Everybody will hang on to a handwritten thank-you note.

Strategy 9

Support your staff.

Phyllis: You asked what I do for my staff. One of my parents, a dad, had a massage chair and did massages. Cathy went through cancer, and when she passed away, we had him come right to the school and give the teachers chair massages. That was probably one of the best things that I ever did for my staff. I also hired someone to come in and talk to us about grieving for Cathy while she was going through that year. I think that was something that brought us all together. We all went to her house often and visited her. I think that was one of the hardest times we ever went through. Having the professionals, the social workers, come and work with us, I think that was a strength.

Julie: That's so touching. I can see why you guys have been voted the best preschool in Waltham for so many years. Is there anything you would like to say in closing, Phyllis?

Phyllis: Julie, I think you're doing a wonderful job. I think the new directors and old directors and all the teachers are so lucky to have you as part of their lives. I think without you, we would not be doing the best job we can do. We thank you for all your time you've given to the organization.

Julie: Thank you so much. I worked with you guys several years ago, probably before that.

Phyllis: I think it was before accreditation began. We had such a wonderful time. We have very fond memories of you. You motivated our staff then, and you're still motivating our staff. We really thank you for it and love you for all you do.

Julie: Thank you. I love you guys too. Please give my best to everybody at your organization. Phyllis Regan, thank you so much for joining us here as we help child care programs and preschools pursue greater levels of child care business success.

Update: In 2016, The Carousel School was named Waltham's best preschool for the nineteenth consecutive year.

To hear this interview in its entirety, go to **www.ChildCareBusinessSuccess BookVault.com**. The password is **RockMyChildCare.com**.

Chapter 9

Make It Easy—
Keep It Simple and
Experience GROWTH

Featuring Patrick Brown,
Children's Lighthouse

*"Simplicity is the final achievement. After one has
played a vast quantity of notes and more notes, it is
simplicity that emerges as the crowning reward of art."*

Frederic Chopin

When we got on the phone for our interview for this book, Patrick Brown stated that the key to his company's success has always been, right from the very start, hiring incredibly talented people who did things better than he did. These words just rolled off his tongue as he shared that it's that easy. Children's Lighthouse is a franchise with thirty-seven centers. The Brown brothers brought the vision for Children's Lighthouse to fruition with ease and grace in 1997, by opening the first center in Grand Prairie, Texas.

This story is unlike any other story in this book, because it's about a man deciding that he wanted to start a child care business and then convincing his brother that it was a great idea and he should be his partner. Well, the two brothers agreed to be partners, and their child care business was off and running. Yes, two men made a decision to start a child care business . . . with no child care experience.

Mike flirted with the idea of opening a child care company in the mid-1990s, when he gave financial backing to various real estate development ventures, including child care. When he caught his first glimpse into the child care world, he was intrigued. He began doing research, including visiting child care companies across the country.

Once the Brown brothers decided that they were opening a child care program, the question came into play, "What do we name our child care business?" That too seemed to come pretty easily to the Brown brothers. During a family vacation, one family member commented about a lighthouse they saw, and they thought, "Yes, that would make a great name." So with a little creativity, the concepts of a lighthouse were worked into company branding. You'll see in their company logo that a lighthouse takes the place of the letter *I*. Pretty clever, right?

The two businessmen, Mike and Patrick Brown, found themselves in this industry that primarily consists of women, and also found themselves growing attached to an amazing business that cares and nurtures other people's children.

Children's Lighthouse has been named among the Best Places to Work by both the Dallas and San Antonio business journals, and has received a Franchise 500 designation by *Entrepreneur* magazine due to its stability, financial strength and growth. Children's Lighthouse is the leading values-based educational child care system in the United States, employing approximately two hundred fifty people between its company headquarters and eight company-owned centers.

Keep reading as Pat shares some of the secrets of the company's success.

Julie: How did you get started? How did Children's Lighthouse come into fruition?

Pat: It was through my brother. Financially he'll participate and back different companies and different projects. It was real estate related. He was potentially going to back a builder financially. It was for a group that technically went into shopping centers. He looked at the program and wasn't totally wild about the venture, but he was intrigued by the industry, I suppose. He spent a couple of years researching the industry and decided we'd do a start-up. I was working for a company at the time, and he asked me if I wanted to participate. I did my own homework. Then I said, "Yeah, let's do the deal." It was basically a start-up, and that's how we got started. I guess we got our first center in Grand Prairie. We were actually going with a franchisor. That was the motive. We found the site and bought it. At the last minute, the bank was uncomfortable with the franchisor. We had a quick decision to make. We decided to go ahead and proceed. We could have gone ahead with another franchisor, but we were out of time. We pulled the trigger, so to speak, and decided to do it.

Julie: So that would be one that you would own?

Pat: Yes, the first one we owned. I don't think we had any grand plans of putting in lots of centers or even franchising. It was just a venture, and we thought we'd give it a try and see if it's something we liked. We got into it and liked it very much. It's a business, but it's an emotional business. If you go to a burger place and you get a bad burger, you'll probably go back. There's not much emotional attachment. In child care, this is people's most precious item on earth. It's a very different business from that standpoint. After getting involved, we just really liked it. It's a warm environment. You go to the centers and look in the classrooms, and all the children are smiling. It's a happy place. It's still a for-profit business, but we got involved and liked it, enjoyed it.

As time went on, we decided that we'd put in more centers. We grew internally organically. We were thinking about franchising, but we weren't going to be that aggressive about it. We were busy doing what we were doing. Then we had our competitors. You can go look online and get the FDD (franchise disclosure document). We were trying to review FDDs and learn a bit more about the franchising side of it. We'd made a decision that we were probably going to do it, but we weren't prepared to do it immediately. We were leaning in that direction. And then we had a gentleman who had researched other franchisors and was familiar with our centers. He came in and said he wanted to be our first franchisee. We said, "Well, Don, we're not ready yet." He was a very sophisticated guy, had plenty of capital, or we probably wouldn't have done it. He just said, "I know where you are and what you're doing. I'll just work with you and work through this first deal together." We said okay. He knew going in what we were doing. If it had been someone less sophisticated, we wouldn't have done it. He understood it. We understood it. And he was really pushing us, more than we were trying to push the program.

That's kind of how it got started. We grew slowly. We're a pretty conservative company. We just wanted to make sure that we had everything in place and worked out all the bugs, or whatever we needed to work out. That's kind of how we got started in the franchising side of it. Currently we still manage our own centers. Our primary focus, from a growth perspective, is on the franchise side of it. We brought in some people, probably five, six years ago. Jessica Stone was a franchise administrator for other companies. She was just wonderful and helped us evolve from what was basically a mom-and-pop program. After that we brought in Steve Dixon, who has been in the business forever, at least twenty years, on the franchising side of it. Jessica kind of got us started, from an organizational standpoint, and then Stephen came in and put it on steroids. He's very, very good at what he does. He transformed us from our mom-and-pop program into a well-run small company. That's kind of how we got started and how we got to where we are. Every year we constantly evolve and try to improve things and make things better.

Julie: You guys started in 1997, was it?

Pat: I believe '97 was our first center. It's been about seventeen years.

Julie: How many do you own personally right now, that are not franchised?

Pat: We have eight right now that we operate.

Julie: In 1997 we have two young, good-looking brothers who say, "Let's open up a child care program." You said there was some homework that went along with you making this decision. What was it in your mind that sparked the idea that child care would be a good idea? It's such a different venture from probably anything you'd done before. So what kind of homework did you do to come to the conclusion to open up child care programs?

Pat: It was really my brother, quite frankly. It was pretty much his deal. He did a lot of homework. Some of these companies were public. He went and visited different companies all over the country, looked at their operations. I think he was intrigued by the industry.

I think the more he got involved in it, the more he learned, and the more he liked it. It's a family-run company, so we're very family-oriented anyway. I think it just ended up being a good fit for us. It's something that I'd never dreamed of prior to this, and I'm sure he hadn't either. As far as employee-based, it's primarily a female industry. There are some males in it, but in general it's a female organization.

Julie: We usually have the women who start the company and then the husbands get dragged in to do the books.

Pat: That's primarily it. Even with our franchisees, I think the men are more involved on the business side of it. From an operational standpoint, it's pretty much a female-dominated industry, which we hadn't really been in before. It was wonderful. Like I say, most of our company is females. They're very bright, very smart and very loyal. We've been very fortunate from that standpoint. There was a lot of research that went into it, and he really liked it. He asked me if I was interested, so I did my own homework and said, "Yeah, let's do it." We were probably fortunate on the front end of the deal that we had a good director. If we had picked one who wasn't as good, it could have been a big detriment to our company. It all worked out, and here we are today.

Julie: Did you have any concerns being two men coming into a predominately female industry?

Pat: Not really. When we first got started, we were in the centers all the time. We were in the office some, but there wasn't a great amount to do, as we were growing other than the real estate side of it. We were in the centers and understood the operational side of it. In the large companies, you've got KinderCare and Children's World. There are plenty of males, I guess more on the corporate side of it. For the operations side of it, it is primarily female. We didn't really have a concern of that. It's a different business than a standard business, because, like I said, you're dealing with children. The customers have a very emotional attachment to the service we provide. It's different from that standpoint, but we're very comfortable in that environment too. It just really wasn't a major issue for us.

Julie: Being two brothers, this started as a family business. It sounds like you brought more family into the picture.

Pat: Correct.

Strategy 1

Have job descriptions.

Julie: Were there boundaries or guidelines that you purposefully put into place to help keep it professional, to not let work run into your personal lives, or just so that it was a happy situation for everyone?

Pat: You have job descriptions. We try to adhere to those job descriptions. I think you start out from that perspective. Family businesses are family businesses. Some are run much better than others. I think we've done a pretty good job with trying to keep the business side of it business, and the family side of it family.

Julie: So you try to keep it separate from each other.

Pat: Yeah. It can be challenging at times, but that's just kind of how it is.

Julie: So your brother won't come in complaining about Aunt Mary?

Pat: No, we try to keep everything— Family is family. We're a close family. I think we all know the boundaries. We understand it is a business, and we're a for-profit business. We need to run it like a business. The family side of it, that's another issue. We think we've done a pretty good job so far, but you just have to stay on top of it.

Julie: Are there any things you would recommend to people not to do when it comes to working with family? If we were to make a "do not do" list, are there things you've learned or discovered?

Pat: I think it's really just, coming in, you have to have a job description of basically what it is you're going to do.

Julie: Clearly defined rules?

Pat: I think so. If you can stay in that arena. If you want to learn something else, that's great. Get one thing out of the way. Being a small business, we all wear different hats anyway. You kind of have your day job. In a small company, it's not what you want to do. It's what needs to get done. You have to keep that in mind. If you're working in this environment, you just know that whatever needs to get done, you get it done. If it's late at night, on the weekend, it doesn't make any difference. You take care of business. I would say get some clearly defined job descriptions, and everyone make everyone accountable for doing their job.

Julie: That's great. Where did the name Children's Lighthouse come from? How did you conceptualize that?

Pat: It happened very quickly. We decided to do the independent program, and we didn't have a name. You had to incorporate, so I had no idea what names we were even looking at. We had to have a name. I think it might have been my mother who came up with it. I think she was with my brother and his young children on a trip to the coast or whatever, and there were some lighthouses. We checked with the government entity to find out if the name was taken. It wasn't taken, so we jumped on it. I'm pretty sure that's how it came about.

Julie: It's probably been great for branding and really standing out as a different place.

Pat: It just worked out perfectly. It's just something else that was not planned. We basically had to have a name and didn't have a clue what to call it. We were under time restraints, obviously. As a corporate entity, we had to have something for it to move forward.

Strategy 2
Find a model.

Julie: That's fantastic. When you were first starting out and thinking, *Here's our first center, we've got the name, we're getting things in a row*, were there any marketing challenges that you faced?

Pat: There were. We kind of knew what our competitors do. Our director had worked for our competitor. Within the industry, a lot of people do the same things from a marketing perspective. We had a template anyway. From there, you just evolve. I think we started out similar to what our competitors do, or the ones we thought were formidable, good competitors. We pretty much knew what they did. The teachers we hired, they'd worked for other companies too, so they were familiar with it also. We already came in doing a lot of things right to begin with, just because it's a mature industry. It's not a new industry. The people who do direct mail, they have a lot of customers who are child care operators as well, so they gave us advice too. We were fortunate on the front end that we already came in with a marketing program. We did a lot of research prior to opening the doors anyway. We were pretty much ahead of it. From there you just evolve anything and everything. Sometimes you try things and they don't work as well. You look at the cost factor, if you get much for your return. Some are yes and some no. You stick with the ones that you do get a return on. We started out with probably a pretty good program anyway, but it evolves.

Strategy 3

Stay competitive with your rates and wages.

Julie: What do you think is one of the biggest marketing "oops, we wouldn't do that again"?

Pat: I'll tell you what we did, not so much from a marketing standpoint, but we were trying to increase enrollment. This was at our McKinney, Texas, center. This was probably ten years ago, maybe twelve years ago. We thought if we reduced our tuition rates, it would increase our enrollment. It didn't. All it did was go straight to the bottom line. We didn't really increase enrollment. All we did was reduce our tuition rate. This was in the very early stages. We brought in some managers from the big companies, KinderCare and Children's World, and, of course, the first thing they said was, "Do not do that. Your competitors across the street are probably going to say, 'Okay, they're not good enough, so they have to reduce their rates.'" We never even looked at it like that. It made perfect sense. It's something that we tried. It's probably just because we were so new to the industry, we just didn't know any better.

Julie: I think a lot of people do that. They think, *If we just lower our rates, we'll attract more people.*

Pat: It made sense to us at the time, but anyone who had been in the child care industry would have known better.

Julie: It's something I still hear from child care owners, and really any entrepreneur. "When business is suffering or we need more, let's make it less so we attract more." What is your current philosophy with rates? Are you competitive? Are you above competition? Do you believe in being the highest price because you offer the best? What is your philosophy when it comes to setting your rates?

Pat: All markets are different. We go off strict demographics when we do site selection. Prior to going in on our site selection program, we already know what the rates are in the market. If it's a market that will dictate the rates we need to have in order to be profitable, we go into that market. If they don't, we don't. We know who our primary competitors are, and we're pretty much in line with them.

Julie: So your rates determine your location, where you will or won't go?

Pat: Very much so. You have a pro forma. We know what the costs of the projects are. We know what tuition rates they'll have to have in order to make a profitable entity. That's all done way ahead of time, before we ever go into a market. I guess to answer your question, we go in and know who our competitors are. We're all pretty much on the same price line.

Julie: So you stay competitive with what you offer.

Pat: Very much so. All the rates aren't the same. We're in different markets, and they will vary. A lot of it is dictated off what our existing competitors are doing.

Julie: Does the same philosophy apply when it comes to staff and what you pay them?

Pat: It does to a certain degree. We have a real good idea, because there are ways to find out what our competitors are paying, so we do the same thing.

Julie: You go in there and just make sure you're competitive with what you're offering?

Pat: Very much so.

Julie: I think one of the biggest motivators for staff is opportunities for growth. How have you put that into practice in your program?

Strategy 4

Promote from within.

Pat: Anytime we have the opportunity to promote within, we do. They already know our system. They already know what we do and how we do it. It's much easier to bring somebody up. The ladies are very good at assessing the personnel in the centers, and who they think is possibly promotable. That's our first choice. If it's a certain center in a certain area, and we don't think the person within our system is ready, then we go outside. It works fine too, but our preference is most definitely to hire from within and train them and monitor them. That's just the philosophy we've had since we've been in business.

Julie: So starting out as a small, one-center program and growing to all these numbers, more than thirty, that you have today, I think of the saying, "You have to let go to grow."

Pat: Correct.

Julie: That is scary for many leaders. You are probably the ultimate in letting go, because you have created. You don't own the centers. You franchise them out. What are some things that you personally have implemented, so that you let go so you can grow?

Pat: I think it's more personnel related. I think it's a matter of being fortunate enough to have brought in the right people for the right positions. Like I said, we just wear a bunch of different hats. We've been fortunate enough, as we've grown, to have done most all of these things anyway. Steve had been in the business twenty years, and Jessica had been in it five or six. They had much more experience than us, at least on the franchise side of the business. For us it was wonderful because we had an opportunity to see what someone can do who's been in the industry a long time. We had not been in the industry a long time. It started by a guy saying he wanted to be our first franchisee. We weren't ready. We didn't know a great amount about franchising at the time. We went to an IFA conference, International Franchise Association, in D.C. ten years ago or whatever, just trying to get some ideas. We talked to some of our competitors in the child care business. They were nice and forthcoming. We said, "We're little guys, and we're thinking about doing this." That was really helpful, because then we got names and phone numbers. We said, "If we have a few questions, would you mind visiting with us?" They all said, "No, not a problem. We're competitors, but we're all in the same business and dealing with children." That was very helpful to us.

I guess to answer your question, as we grew, we had the cash flow to hire people who were more experienced than us at the time. We stumbled through it. It was more of a mom-and-pop deal until we brought in someone. We had different jobs. We had a thousand other things going at the time too. We couldn't spend 100 percent of our time working on FDDs, selling and so on. It's been transforming to bring people in and see how good they are in an arena that we were learning as we were going. It's been great for us to watch the transition. We try to promote internally. Some of the people here, they've been with us a long time. We have a new vice president of operations, but she's been with us seven years now. Steve has been promoted also. For us, if we can promote internally the people who have the skills, who have done it for a long time . . . We just didn't have the experience level they had. For us, it frees us up a little bit to do things that we need to do also.

Strategy 5

Hire people better than you.

Julie: So you're saying hire people who are better at doing those things than you are.

Pat: Very much so. We can get through the program, but they've done this for many years. There's no way we're going to learn in months what they've learned over twenty years. We just don't have the time to do it, and have other duties we have to do also. Even on the operations side, we were small. What helped us is we brought in people who had worked for the big companies. It was a win-win for us. We were smaller and didn't have as many organizational things in place, processes. They had to do all of that for years at the big companies. We loved it because they could come in and help us establish more processes. They liked it because they had a lot more freedom here than they would have had at a big company. If there's an issue, they can pick up the phone, and we can make a really quick decision. The large companies, you have to go through five people to get something done. They've told us this. For us, it's a win-win. We brought in some very experienced process-oriented people. For them, it was great because they have much more freedom within our system. We're small and can get things done immediately, whereas they couldn't do it in the big company. It's worked for us having people come from the larger companies into a smaller company.

Julie: They were immediately able to take more ownership of what was going on, feeling like an entrepreneur themselves at times.

Pat: We have a very inclusive management environment. We have meetings. They're not long, but we have an agenda. They're very much involved in it. There's clearly a chain of command, but, at the same time, we very much listen to what their views are. Most of the time, if it makes sense, we go with their suggestions.

Julie: Looking back at everything you've experienced since opening your child care franchise, what is one of the biggest challenges you recall?

Pat: I think in the early days, when we started selling more, just having the personnel and the manpower to do some things. We were prepared for them, but I think it's something that, just growing and maybe not having the personnel at the right time . . . We quickly got that cured. I think a lot of it is processes. It takes a lot of time, energy and money to make things simple. I think we've done a very good job at that. You want to make sure the franchisee understands exactly what they're getting into. At this point, we've done a really good job. We change our FDD yearly. Through the year, if we get comments on this, this, this and this, then we try to address all these issues so there's no misunderstanding from our customer, on the franchisor side of it. From a challenging perspective, I think it's trying to make things simple and understandable. It's a constant effort that we work on yearly.

Strategy 6

Keep it simple.

Julie: I like the words you're using, especially the word *simple*. You used that one a couple of times. A lot of people say it's hard. How do you get to the mindset where you're trying to develop this vision based on it being simple?

Pat: If something is complicated, if we don't understand it internally, then the franchisees are certainly not going to understand it. We've all come to the agreement that we want to make it simple.

Everyone in the company is very focused on *Do we understand this?* If we don't, then we need to make it much more clear. I think it's just companywide. Everybody thinks like that.

Julie: Keep simplifying. That's good. I think that's a really powerful strategy in itself.

Pat: The last thing you want is someone who does not understand what we're trying to do. Like I said, it takes time, money and effort to make things simple. I think we've done a good job at it.

Julie: I think simplicity also comes with systems and processes.

Pat: It does. Steve is probably the best process person I've ever been involved with. I've worked for different companies, and he's very process-oriented. He's naturally like that. Then you have the benefit of him working for other, larger companies, where they have plenty of processes in place. It may take me a month to do something he could probably do in two days, because he's good at it.

Julie: "Here are the ten steps, and now we've got them documented and laid out."

Pat: That's it. It makes everybody accountable. Even internally, if we have the processes in place, then whoever is doing it, there's accountability also. It makes it much easier if there's a process to it. The processes all evolve. We change our processes as we go. We hope for the better, and I think it is for the better.

Julie: Now that you are the president of Children's Lighthouse, what does an average day look like for you, or is there no average day?

Pat: There is no average day. You come in and check e-mails. Half of them are junk, so you've got to dig through the pertinent ones. I guess checking e-mails kind of dictates the agenda for the day. From there, it's what's up that day, and then things arise. There isn't a typical day really, especially when you're a smaller company. Whatever the major issue is of the day, that's what we get addressed.

Julie: Did you ever spend any time in a classroom, teaching?

Pat: I have not done the teaching. I'm not sure they'd want me in there. I'll tell you a quick story. One of our centers in McKinney, it was open six months. We have cameras in all of our classrooms. I walked into the infant room. We had two phone calls, both of them, "Who's that guy in there?" Not that male teachers are a problem. The customer just has a perception, right or wrong, of who a teacher should be. As far as going in and teaching, that's one of the few things we have not done. I think it's for maybe practical reasons. Parents typically want to see the teacher who's going to be in there full time. They get very attached to the teachers, the parents do. I've sat in, but I have not technically taught.

Julie: So one day, it led to a couple of questions and phone calls asking, "Who is this person?"

Pat: You can go to the Internet, and only the people who are enrolled can get to the cameras. You bet they watch them. They just wanted to know who I was. That day it was a construction-related issue, something with the air conditioning. I was out in the area and the repairman said, "See if cold air is coming out," something to that effect. I just stopped in and looked in the classroom. Our customers do use that webcam service.

Julie: They just proved it to you that day. If you're talking to somebody who's thinking about going into the child care industry, what advice would you offer them?

Pat: I would offer them the advice of, "Go with the franchisor." We were probably lucky. Some things fell into place for us, and we were fortunate to have a competent director. If we hadn't been that fortunate, we could have gotten into trouble really quickly, not from a safety issue or the children not being provided for, but from a financial standpoint. There are a lot of things you have to know in the child care profession that maybe in some other businesses you don't. There are a lot of rules, a lot of regulations, and you truly have to have the experience to do it. We were fortunate that it worked out okay. If we had made the wrong pick on the front end, we would have struggled. I assume we'd have figured it out sooner or later, but we probably would have struggled. If you don't know this profession, this industry, I would go with a franchisor. Hopefully it's us, but if it isn't, there are good competitors out there that run good companies. I would strongly suggest you go that route, rather than trying to do a start-up on your own. If you've been in the business, and you know the business, and you know the operational side of it, maybe it's a different story. If you have very little experience within the child care industry, I would certainly recommend you go with a franchisor.

Julie: What's a typical investment to purchase a franchise?

Pat: It varies, anywhere from probably two and a half million to three million dollars, depending on what part of the country you go into. Land prices dictate that. Construction prices dictate it, but they don't fluctuate near as much as the land prices do. You'll be in that arena.

Julie: What are some of the strategies, especially early on, that you used to really build those positive relationships with parents?

Pat: I think so much of it is the director you hire at the center. Clearly they have to have the skills to operate the center, and the educational background. I think a lot of it is just rapport and warmth. Having a good curriculum program and managing it well is all important, but I think your director sets the tone on what kind of teachers they hire. We're in a business that is child care. I think you want somebody very warm. We're not in the burger business. With what we do, we're taking care of children. It's somewhat of an emotional-type industry. I think that emotion comes through your director and the people your director hires.

Julie: You bring up the example with the burger. Typically when you order a burger, you don't get a hug.

Pat: If it's not a great burger, you'll probably try them again anyway. If you don't get that feeling from your child care learning center, you may go down the road and find a director you're comfortable with, who smiles, who's warm. A lot of it, I think, starts with your director.

Strategy 7
Know your numbers.

Julie: That's good. I want to go back to numbers for a moment. I know one of the things that comes up a lot in our different child care programs is confidentiality around numbers, or people not wanting to share what numbers are, what budgets are. Sometimes the directors don't have firsthand knowledge of what their budgets are and what they can spend. Is there a certain way you guys manage that, in terms of which numbers you give your downline access to, so that they can make decisions, or so that they can meet goals?

Pat: We have ratios on everything. As far as budgeting, we have ratios. For personnel issues, you have to stay within certain guidelines on a host of different areas. It's very much calculated. We look at all of our franchisees' numbers. We have access to all of their numbers. We look at labor costs. We look at accounts receivable, and a whole host of things. We get on the computer and review numbers weekly. If we see something, we can get on the phone immediately and say, "You need to check this." There are categories that they need to stay within certain ratios and budgets on.

Julie: Do the directors in organizations typically know what all the budget numbers are?

Pat: Oh, yes.

Julie: I know sometimes there's a bit of hesitancy to share numbers, but then it can make it difficult to achieve goals, if you don't really know what's going on.

Pat: They have all the numbers. I'm not sure how they could do their job if they didn't have the numbers, or that's how we feel anyway.

Julie: I definitely agree with that. What is the vision that guides you every single day to continue on with Children's Lighthouse and to make it bigger and keep growing?

Pat: I think it's just the love of the industry. We're passionate about children. We're passionate about learning. It fits into what we do, the business side of it. Clearly we want to grow. We want to be the best operator in the country. I think it's more the reason we got into it. We did our original homework and research. It ended up being a good fit for us. We hadn't been sure it would be, but since we got into it, the passion hasn't waned for us. The children side of it is very important. The learning is very important also. I think it's really the vision we've had from day one. We're passionate about what we're doing, and I believe our franchisees are also.

Julie: Fantastic. Is there anything that you do to stay motivated on a daily or weekly basis?

Pat: I think when we come into the office, we're motivated. I think I feed off other people. I think Steve Dixon said it the best. We were having a conversation about a year ago, and he said he feeds off the emotions of everybody else. I said, "I do too." We're a small company, but we have a lot of people who are passionate about what they do. I think everybody feeds off each other's passion.

Julie: If someone were to ask you how your program differs from all others that are out there, what would you tell them?

Pat: This is just coming from our franchisees who sign up. We ask them, "Why did you pick us?" I think we have a much more family environment. I know we're smaller, but it is a family-owned company. I think they know we're engaged in the business. I think they know we have passion for the business. They know we're very accessible. We tell them constantly, "If you have a problem, pick up the phone. You can call any of us. If it's in the operations arena, if I can answer it, then I will certainly answer it. If not, I will get someone on the phone immediately and get you in touch with who you need to speak with." I think there's much more of a family environment for what we do, as opposed to our competitors. That's what they've told us. It's a business, but we try to keep it light. We try to keep a family environment, as opposed to a corporate structure.

Strategy 8

You are a community business.

Julie: Who is important for you to network with in the community? Do you still network with your competitors, or are you more involved with other business organizations now?

Pat: I think probably more business organizations. We're a community business. Even on a marketing strategy, those can vary from market to market. Our primary market is probably a three- to five-mile radius. We're very much a community business. You want to be involved with everything in your community, everything and anything. I think you want to be involved with the chamber of commerce, the school districts. You are a community business. Like I said, we're in the child care business. It's even that much more important that people know who we are, and what we do, and that we're passionate about it. I think it's very important that we do the community marketing and stay involved with everybody in the community, because that is our market. They're not driving twenty miles to come to one of our centers. They're driving one to four miles, and that's it. From a community perspective, we are involved in our communities. If we can do things from a charitable standpoint, we do. We're a community business, and that's what we have to pursue. Everyone does a pretty good job at it.

Julie: I often advise child care owners to play a bigger game, to rise to the level where people in the community can see them, and see them as the child care expert. Are you out there speaking at chamber meetings?

Pat: It varies from community to community, but any community involvement you can do is important. We have a fall festival also. It's kind of like a Halloween deal. We have a Mardi Gras parade at one of our centers. Anything and everything involving the community, charity. We do drives. We sent a bunch of goods down to West, Texas, after an explosion there. We have a great public relations firm that gives us ideas on how we can help within any community. We're very focused on that.

Strategy 9:
Give back.

Julie: Was giving back something that you decided early on you wanted to be a part of, or was it something where you thought, *This will help propel us and, at the same time, help more people*?

Pat: I think it came about as we got a little larger. I think in the early stages, you're so covered up with basically taking care of business, opening centers. As we've matured, we thought it was very important. We have a list of charities that we give to. We were involved with the Ronald McDonald House and the Navy SEALS program, the wounded veterans. We have a list of things. That's evolved too. I think as of last year, we were working with Cook Children's Hospital, where people who come into town, if they don't have the money and one of their children is in the hospital, we give them free child care at our Risinger center. We give brothers and sisters a place to go, rather than just staying in the hospital with mommy and daddy. We try to do things that we think will help from a children's perspective also.

Julie: One of the ways I've seen Children's Lighthouse be so different than anybody else is there are constant articles, constant social media, about the different things you're involved with. You're always seeing the kids putting in the cans for the Ronald McDonald House, or whatever it is. There is always publicity around those things.

Pat: I think it's something that we want to be known for, helping the community in any way we can.

Julie: When it comes to employee benefits, I hear a lot about child care programs debating whether or not to give free child care to staff. What is your philosophy around that?

Pat: It's changed through the years. Currently I think we give, for teachers, tuition rate at 50 percent.

Julie: I was studying different business models. I was fascinated with the child care industry, because it's the only industry where I hear about people just giving away the service for free in some cases. I always question, "Is that a good business model? You don't go to a grocery store and say, 'If you work here, you get so many groceries for free.'"

Pat: We chose to do it. It's evolved through the years. I think at one time we did 100 percent for free. It also may depend on if the center is full or if it isn't full. If the space is available, why not let one of our staff members have the slot at a discount? I just think there's no reason not to. They work every day. We prefer to help them.

Julie: Are there any other special benefits offered, let's say if you have a teacher who doesn't have children?

Pat: No, I think it's just pretty much compensation.

Julie: I think that's pretty much standard in this industry too.

Pat: What is different in this industry, just the way the industry is structured, we typically pay more than our competitors, as far as wages. It's a business where the people who want to be in child care *want* to be in child care. You can go from one burger place to the next. You just get twenty cents more per hour. Most of the people in child care, they choose to be in it, which is different from a minimum-wage job. They want to be in child care, and that's very important.

Julie: Absolutely. I know that you guys have done a lot of different team-building activities over the years. Is there a moment with your entire staff that was just a total unity process, or fun process, that everybody went through together as a team?

Pat: We do a Kids Rock, which I think we do every year. It's at a skating rink. We have multiple things we do. It varies from market to market.

Julie: Is there one moment in all your years of doing this that has just really touched your heart, that stands out, that makes it all worth it?

Pat: It's on a daily basis. I don't think there's one incident that stands out. We've been in the business a long time. We get stuck in the office a lot of times up here, just doing the business side of the business. I make myself get out and go to the centers. You realize what we're in business for. We're a for-profit company, but you go out there, and it's just such a warm environment. The directors are nice. They smile. The teachers are warm. The kids are happy. I think on a daily basis, it's a warm, nice industry. We're providing a wonderful service. Following our curriculum, the children will go into school probably two years academically ahead of their peers who don't follow our curriculum. We're just providing a service where we're getting them started in life, hopefully in the right way. It's rewarding on a daily basis.

Julie: That's what makes this industry so fantastic. It's not just that one moment. It's, like you said, everyday moments.

Strategy 10

Decorate—a lot!

Pat: We decorate a lot. It's part of the theme. Some of our competitors don't, but we believe in it, and we like it. Any holiday you can imagine, whether it be Fourth of July, Columbus Day, there are things on the walls. They're educational-related, but they're fun. We want our centers to be warm. We don't want them to look like doctors' offices. We want them looking like child care. It's certainly a learning center, but we want to make sure that it's a very warm, inviting environment. The ladies do a great job on decorating the rooms. Every holiday you can imagine, they're decorated with something.

To hear this interview in its entirety, go to **www.ChildCareBusinessSuccess BookVault.com**. The password is **RockMyChildCare.com**.

Chapter 10

It All Comes Back to Your People

Featuring Ty Durekas, Children's Creative Learning Centers

"You don't build a business. You build people— and then people build the business."

Zig Ziglar

I picked up the phone to chat with Ty Durekas shortly after I was referred to him by one of our sponsors, Simon Ho with ChildCareIRiS. Simon raved about this man who has opened hundreds of child care programs and experienced tremendous success. I was told about the passion that he had for child care, and if there was anyone I was going to feature in this book, it should be Ty.

Talking with Ty, I immediately knew Simon was right. This man knew his stuff, and additionally was gracious and willing to share when I told him what this project was all about. He sat on our panel at the first annual Child Care Business Success Conference in Chicago, where he shared his story, and a wealth of information, about opening and operating not just one successful child care business, but more than 1,800 of them!

During our interview Ty stated, "If someone had asked me a week prior (to my making the decision to open up a preschool), 'Do you know you're going to be opening a preschool in sixty days?,' I would have thought they were crazy."

So how did his journey begin? It was a whim. A whim to open up a child care program. Ty admits that if he thought about doing now what he and his wife, Fran—then his girlfriend—did twenty years ago, he might not do it. But he was in his early twenties at the time and "appropriately naïve." He was willing to take risks.

Once he and Fran—who had a teaching credential and had started an afterschool program at Stanford University—decided to open a preschool, they searched for a location. They found a building that had been boarded up, and had only forty-five days to get it ready to open in August 1992. All the while, Ty continued his day job. He was working eighty hours a week.

Within three months, that first Children's Creative Learning Center in Sunnyvale, California, had a full program. A second program was opened within six months. Ty and Fran grew the organization to about twenty programs, always remembering not to neglect the existing programs while preparing to open a new one.

How did they do it? Well, here's what Ty told me. "I think really what occurred in that situation is we believed. I think it comes down to belief. We didn't have children, but we believed that if we created a positive environment for staff, and a quality environment for children, and we charged more, we could create a quality child care program."

And so they did.

As Ty's passion for the industry deepened, he worked with various communities and employers to develop child care programs throughout Silicon Valley. Employers included Google and Cisco. Cisco grew to two onsite child care programs, which now serve more than 25,000 employees.

"What makes your program successful?" is the question that Ty continuously asks child care owners as he travels the world, researching other child care centers. Even if he doesn't speak the native language, he asks that same question. In every language, the answer is the same: The teachers. His belief—that if a child care program has a positive environment for staff, and a quality environment for children, then the program will be a success—is consistently revalidated by child care owners worldwide.

I'm delighted to share with you a portion of my interview with Ty Durekas.

Julie: Why don't we start with a little bit of your journey? How did you get into the child care industry?

Ty: Well, it was actually completely by happenstance. My wife, who was my girlfriend at the time, and I had started conversations about early childhood, because she was a teacher and had a teaching credential and had started an afterschool program at Stanford University. As we were talking one time around the kitchen table, as we did often, I said, "Why don't we open a preschool together?" That resulted in us finding a location that had been boarded up, and putting a lot of sweat and tears and time into getting this location up and running. It took about forty-five days. This was in June of 1992.

For those forty-five days, basically I was working two jobs, my day job and then my night job.

We opened the school in August. We focused on three principal areas, and felt this was going to drive real success in developing a new child care organization. One was retaining the best possible people we could get. Two was charging on the higher end of the tuition scale for the area. Three was focusing on quality. We wanted to make sure that the programs were set up to meet quality standards. We invested in teachers on the upper end of the pay scale. What resulted was we ended up with very, very loyal staff who stayed with us for almost the twenty years that we owned the business, fifteen staff members to be exact. What was really nice about the whole process was that we watched them develop and grow in their roles. Many of them moved on to be directors, and even vice presidents, within the organization as we grew it. I think it's a really nice story about CCLC, the company I started, Children's Creative Learning Centers, with Fran. We started with one program. We grew the organization to about twenty programs. I also want to mention that Fran and I could never have accomplished what we did if it wasn't for the countless numbers of wonderful people who we worked with. Cindy O'Mara and Deepa MacPherson are two people who were most instrumental during the entire journey. Both of these ladies held numerous roles and through their passion and wisdom we built CCLC into a beautiful organization.

So twenty years in the business, but fifteen years owning CCLC. The most immense joy I've gotten out of that process of growing an organization was watching the staff evolve and mature professionally and personally, and also having families come back and visit us over the years, and the children who were now going on to college. It was a really tough and interesting feeling, knowing that you're getting older and seeing some of the children you had when they were three or four years old heading off to college. That's kind of a recap of my background.

Julie: What a legacy to leave too, of the work that you've done in this industry. I always emphasize growing your staff, but to see the kids grow, to see your staff grow, and to see these people becoming vice presidents of the organization, what an incredible gift to give to so many people. Recently I was with one of my clients, and we did a professional development program, two days with the top leadership team, and then one day with the entire staff. Just the profound moment of seeing this owner standing in front of his entire staff and thinking, *Look at all these people who are employed because of what we created. Look at all these people who have more in their lives because of this business that we created.* When we talk about business and success, it's such a profound thing.

Ty: I agree with you. One of the wonderful parts about creating a business like this is, I'm a social entrepreneur. I believe that this sort of a business is so valuable because you're working with children ages zero to five. You're helping them in the most foundational and most important years of their lives, before they even go to kindergarten. You're helping them basically get prepared and have their first, in many cases, socialized experiences. You're helping also these families with their parenting. Many of them are new parents, so they rely on a child care center to help them with some of the common challenges, like biting and other things that occur with young children. That has also been very personally rewarding for me, to watch my own knowledge develop over time.

Let your staff shine.

The other thing that I would say to child care operators who are operating even one center is that if you have staff who are there for a long time, one of the most important things you can do is help them to further develop. Give them additional opportunities to help you be successful as an organization. I watched teachers who went from assistant teachers, to teachers, to lead teachers. Then from lead teachers, they were responsible for maybe managing all of the preschool programming or creating the curriculum. Even in one location, a child care center operator arrangement, you can create opportunities for your staff. I think that's very, very important to retaining them.

Turnover rates are so high. Most staff that I've talked to over the years really want to be respected professionally. They want to be appreciated and respected. I think everybody who might read this would acknowledge that child care staff do not get paid what engineers get paid. They do not get paid what other professionals, like lawyers or doctors, might get paid. The work they do is equal to, if not more important than, some of those other professions, because they're dealing with children. They're the future of our society. I think making people feel appreciated, having events, recognizing their anniversaries with the organization, acknowledging their birthdays, making them feel respected as professionals by giving them staff development opportunities, are all important.

Julie: I just want to highlight this, because I think it is so key. We've been teaching staff motivation for seventeen years. What you're saying about the respect and appreciation is so important, but it's not like donuts on Friday. It's about your belief in your staff, and not being threatened in any way by their growth. A lot of times I hear, "Oh, they think they're going to be a center director. They think they're going to be an owner." I'm like, "Let them! Train them to be in your shoes. If they open up another center, great. If not, you've got somebody who is really, profoundly impacted by your positive belief in who they are. Your dedication to helping them grow professionally is one of the most amazing things you can give to them."

Strategy 2
Teach your staff your secrets.

Ty: I would agree. Some of you who read this will think, *Gosh, if I went ahead and trained this person, and taught them all my secret sauce, all the things that have made me successful, then they're going to go off and open a location one block from my school, and all of my children are going to go to their school.* The fear motive is one that—I would really strongly encourage you not to think that way. At the end of the day, if you create a positive, supportive environment for your staff, and you invest in them, here are a variety of possible outcomes.

One is you may decide at some point that you want to transition some of your time and do other things. Maybe you have a growing family, and your life circumstances are changing. You might want some of these people, whom you've developed, to step into a role and manage the child care center you have. Or you may decide you want to open another location. You want to have staff who are loyal to you, because they respect you because you respect them. We had three hundred to four hundred employees at one point, before we sold our organization. Many of them had been with us since they came. They never left. What we did was, even in the toughest of times, we were honest with them. We still respected and appreciated them. When the economy was going downward, we still gave them little notes and told them we appreciated them. It's not about food. I know some of you think, "Oh, we'll just give them sugar."

Julie: I wrote an article about that. Chocolate does not motivate.

Strategy 3
Feed your staff's brains, not their stomachs.

Ty: It's sort of funny, because everyone thinks you have to feed staff. It's really about giving them food for their brain and feeding them emotionally, making them feel supported and appreciated, recognizing them when they have a child that's born, and saying, "How are you? How are you feeling? What's going on with you?" I think, personally, that staff is the most important piece of the puzzle, whether it's the directors or the teachers. Make sure they feel appreciated. Everything else—the parents, you and everything else—is going to be successful if they are successful.

Julie: I so agree with you. One of the things that we've been studying is gossip. We've actually developed some programs around it. I want everybody to hear this. If you're dealing with workplace gossip, a lot of times that happens—especially that negative, drama gossip—because people are not mentally stimulated. They're creating this drama. If you're giving them the opportunity, like Ty is talking about, for growth, that's going to substantially decrease that destructive gossip and drama that's going on in your workplace.

Strategy 4
Create a safe environment for discussion.

Ty: To be candid, I think that gossip and drama will exist in almost every child care center, just by the nature of you have young people who are evolving their maturity, and they're evolving professionally. They are still trying to figure out who they are as people. Because of that, you're going to have situations occur. How we handle drama is critical. In the fifteen years that I owned the business, we didn't have one single lawsuit. We didn't have one disgruntled family sue us. We didn't have any incidents with Child Protective Services that resulted in us being fined or anything like that. Sure, there were some basic licensing violations. Those are almost impossible to avoid at some point in that span of time, but not any major challenge. I think the way you avoid drama and gossip, because I think that topic is a big issue in child care settings, is you have to tackle the big topics that are the undercurrent of the center directly. I think when staff meetings occur—you have new people who come on, and they have their own dramas—talk about the general topics that seem to be the undercurrents of the organization.

For example, if there are some staff who are concerned that other staff are able to show up late, and they feel like they are the ones who are always on time, and how come those other people are not being written up, it's not fair and so on, talk about "What sort of rules are we going to put in place so everybody is treated equally?" I think that is important, creating settings like that where people feel they can have a safe environment to have a discussion. Make it very neutral. Don't have people attacking each other—I think that's the other thing. And also not reacting to all of the comments. It can sometimes be very detrimental if a director, particularly, gets involved in the drama. I think you almost have to, as the director, if you can, hold yourself to a higher standard. You need to be the professional, mature person in the situation. Rise above the drama. If the staff are having a challenge, you're not taking sides or getting involved in it just because you're interested. You need to avoid those things.

Julie: You talked earlier in our conversation about how you feel the director is really—I don't know if you called the director the powerhouse, the power source, you used the word *power*. The directors are very powerful in the child care organization. I think part of really being successful and building your successful team is that you as the owner—if you're the owner/director, or if you have a separate director—have to really stay committed to the vision of what you want to bring into fruition, as opposed to focusing on the drama. Your emotions can fuel both things. I think if you live to that higher standard, and really filter all of your power and energy into your vision, that will lead your team on the right path of where you want to go.

Strategy 5
Don't manage by fear.

Ty: I agree. I think part of what I've seen over the years with directors is some of them get consumed with power. What happens is they don't recognize that they are acting like dictators. They don't recognize that they are acting like people who are in a power position. It's awful. Personally, I've seen uprisings from that.

Julie: I think that's where fear comes up again. That's where we're really feeling like we have to control everything. As opposed to inspiring our team, we get fearful, and we feel we have to control because nobody is doing anything the way we needed them to do it, so then it becomes the dictatorship.

Ty: Yeah. If you start your own center and you're the director, maybe you wanted it your way. You were working somewhere else and said, "I can do it differently. I can do it better." In many cases you can. I think that is one of the wonderful aspects that can come out of starting your own center. You can do things the way you like to do them. But you will have a lot of resentful staff if you try to create an environment of fear. Also, I think the other thing you want to watch out for is if your staff are unhappy, or if your staff are fearful. It will come out and be obvious to parents when they are touring the center. Don't think that parents are not aware when they walk into a classroom. They can feel the energy and sense the fear when a staff person and director basically do not want to maintain eye contact.

Fear will sometimes manifest itself that way. If you're touring the center with your two-year-old child, you don't want to be in that situation where you feel like the child is going to be in a tough spot if they were to enroll in that class.

Strategy 6
Connect with parents' emotions, and watch enrollments grow.

Julie: I think it's important to keep in the forefront of our minds how people buy. People buy from a very emotional point, not necessarily logical. It's really how they feel when they come into your child care program. How do they feel when they go into those classrooms? How do they feel when they're leaving your child care program?

Ty: Exactly. It is a lot about first impressions. Make sure that the lobby, the general area where parents walk in, is inviting, warm. The difference between warm and cold to me is real plants versus plastic plants. It doesn't have to be plants. That was just the analogy I wanted to use. Making someone feel like they're walking into an inviting space, let's put it that way. When the parent tours with the child, there are things I look for. Of course, I'm a seasoned professional. I think a lot of parents are getting this advice now because of social media and through all of the parent blogs that are out there. They are a lot more in tune with what to look for, because they have heard from people like myself and other people to look for these things.

When I walk into a classroom, I look for engagement between the teacher and the director, or the teacher and the person giving me the tour. I look for: Is she welcoming this tour? Is this at a good time? Do they look like they interact positively? I want to see what the dynamics are between the staff. Then I look for the room arrangement.

221

Does it look like an enriching environment? Are the staff engaged? In other words, are the staff at the child's level? Are they down working with the children, or are they standing up with their hands folded? You can tell a lot by looking at a teacher. You can tell whether or not he or she is engaged. Staff engagement is very important.

Another thing I look for is cleanliness. Is the room clean? Is it hygienically clean? There are a lot of environments where, if you have cold season, flu season, some kind of illness that's coming through the center, if it's not cleaned regularly, you should ask about that as a parent. I think parents will be curious about the cleanliness. You want to make sure that your center is cleaned regularly. Don't ask your staff to be the cleaning staff. I want to highly encourage everybody not to do that. That's part of the respect piece we talked about. A lot of these staff, they don't get paid a lot of money, and then you're asking them to be a housecleaner in addition to being a teacher. That is, in my opinion, very disrespectful. I know that a lot of child care centers don't do that. Some do, so discourage that.

Julie: I would rather make all of our staff into our salespeople. That would be my vision, two hundred salespeople raving about the program.

Ty: That's one way to do that, getting the staff to be engaged. If I walk in with my child, and I see happy staff, and I see a great environment, then I'm probably going to be more willing to enroll. You're right—it is about them being salespeople.

Julie: It is. We're always buying or selling something. I'd rather have them out there selling me and who I am. It's getting our staff to that point. What you're giving us are some valuable tips. This is really good stuff. I like what you said when we first started this interview, about retaining staff, charging the higher end of the rates, having a quality program. I want to go back with you those twenty-something years ago. You were sitting at that table, having that conversation with your girlfriend. You were thinking about purchasing this boarded-up building. You made it happen in a matter of, what did you say, forty-five days?

Ty: Yes.

Julie: What were the biggest challenges that you overcame at that point? That is a huge, huge thing to accomplish, to be sitting there talking about it and then having those doors open.

Strategy 7
Make it your goal to get the best staff.

Ty: If someone had said to me a week prior to my sitting down at the kitchen table and saying that I was going to open up a preschool in 45 days, "Do you know you're going to be opening a preschool in a matter of sixty days?," I would have thought they were crazy. I think really what occurred in that situation is we believed. I think it comes down to belief. We didn't have children. We believed that if we created a positive environment for staff, and a quality environment for children, and we charged more, then we could pay our staff as much as possible. That was really the goal. The goal was, "How do we get the best staff?"

I've seen preschool programs all over the world. I've been in countries where I did not speak the language, yet I asked the same question, "What makes your program successful?" They will tell you over and over again—it doesn't matter where you're at, doesn't matter what the environment is—it's the teacher. "I have the most amazing teacher." "The parents love the teacher." "The kids love the teacher." "I love this teacher." We wanted to hire the best staff. What we believed is a little bit corny. We thought a little bit like the movie *Field of Dreams*—if you build it, they will come. I guess we just assumed that if we did the right thing, people would be attracted to what we had built. After forty-five days, it turned out that we were wildly successful. Within three months our program was full, and within six months we opened our second program. People just raved about CCLC. They loved what we had created. They knew that that was where they wanted their children to be. It's the best kind of marketing. It's the marketing that doesn't cost you anything.

Strategy 8
Focus on the top thing that will fill your program.

Julie: Is that your biggest marketing secret? There are lots of things we can do with brochures and this and that. I always believe that if you have the enthusiasm for the vision, and you're just setting it right from the start, and people are so excited, then they're going to come. That's a powerful strategy for you.

Ty: A helpful tip for people who are curious about how to market their programs: I don't personally believe that you need to invest in online advertising.

Julie: Or $20,000 brochures?

Ty: No. In fact, I don't even believe in today's society, for the most part, that you need to have a nice brochure. I think you need to have maybe one sheet of paper. I think in the beginning, if you're just starting a program, you might want to have a little bit of information, but it's going to come down to them coming in and touring and seeing the people. It's going to come down to the people, once again. I've seen beautiful child care centers that big companies have set up, that were really nice looking cosmetically, but the staff were in complete disarray, and no one wanted to enroll in the center. The helpful tip here is this: Once you have your program up and running, make sure to survey your staff and your parents anonymously. I want to emphasize the word *anonymously*. Parents and staff should feel safe to be able to provide information. You may think, *If I give them an anonymous environment to do that, they're going to write negative things.* You would be surprised. We did surveys of staff and parents every year. They were always very positive. Every organization has to learn and grow and evolve things, all the time. There were lots of things we worked on, but we got really good information from our staff and from our parents that way, anonymous surveys. We used SurveyMonkey, which is a common, free survey tool, at its Basic level, that you can use online. I would recommend that to everybody.

Julie: There are so many things that an owner can invest his or her time in. How much do you think an owner is cutting his or her profits by, if not investing in having a motivated staff?

Strategy 9

Get out of the office.

Ty: I think that directors are often shortsighted. Many of them will spend too much time in the office and not enough time in the classroom. A lot of staff will be motivated by several things. One, having some opportunities to develop is important for staff. That's how they feel respected. I believe that staff also feel appreciated if someone comes in and acknowledges their work. So if the director is in the office all the time and comes through only during tours, that becomes obvious, and it doesn't feel to the staff like they're all in it together. I would encourage directors to spend more time in the classrooms observing. Helping and supporting can be very, very powerful in motivating staff. Supportive staff feel like, *I don't want to leave my team high and dry*. The most ineffective staff environments, the most dysfunctional ones, are the ones where several people are sick. In every child care center, there is going to be a flu season, or

225

some kind of cold season, that comes through. The staff get it from the children, and then the staff have to stay home. Then, of course, you have all these problems with staffing. What I've found important is creating an environment where it's a team environment, and making sure people are more careful and not getting sick—washing their hands more, sterilizing their rooms. If everybody is working together, it can lead to a more positive and happy staff as well.

Strategy 10

Investing in your staff results in growing your profits.

Julie: Let's talk to our owners about profits. I've heard this a lot over the past seventeen years, that they really don't have money to invest in their staff when there's low morale and they really need some outside help. They tend to view staff motivation as a luxury. We have to spend thousands of dollars on the sand, or on this or that, but when it comes to their staff, it's a more difficult investment to bring somebody in. Let's say you were to sit down face-to-face with an owner and say, "Listen, your staff are going to take about 50 percent of what you're making in payroll. You should also really think about investing in your staff." What would those numbers look like? What would they be cutting their profits by if they're letting all this dysfunction, which happens in many child care programs, go on? Does that question make sense?

Ty: You raise a very good question. It's an important one.

Julie: These are things that your security cameras do not show you, where you can be more profitable as a business owner. I think a lot of it comes down to your staff. I just want to be as blunt as we possibly can about this, to really help owners see where it's worth investing some of their money.

Ty: I'll say it this way. You think to yourself, *Oh, I have to cut my staff hours. I have to cut my staff pay, because we have fewer children.* What happens is it becomes a cycle. Here's what I would say to you: I ran a very profitable business, and my focus was on staff retention and staff satisfaction. That was the Number One thing. I knew, and you should know this as well, that if you have happy staff, if you have staff that are motivated to be there, your enrollment will go up, your retention of parents and children will go up, you will have more positive engagement with families. If families are upset because they believe the staff are upset, many of them will leave. Sometimes staff leave and take four or five children with them. Think about that for a second. You want your staff to be happy. If a staff member leaves, and goes to a center down the street, those parents have that person's cell phone number. They will ask where she's going. In many cases, they'll go with the staff person. It's the same thing with directors. If directors leave, sometimes staff will follow a director because they have a personal relationship with that person.

I've been to religious-based programs in basements that were not fancy, no sort of fancy resources. What they had, though, was amazing staff. People were beating a door down to try to get into those programs, because it's about staff. They wanted their children to be with a great teacher and learn from that teacher. If I can give any of you any advice today, please respect your staff, and appreciate your staff, and develop your staff. To put it into numbers, if you have occupancy levels below 72 percent, you usually don't make money. You want to have occupancy numbers above 72 percent.

To achieve that, you have to have positive tours. You have to be able to have people come in, and see the environment, and be happy that that's where they want to leave their children. If you invest, let's say, $2,000 on staff development, think about what one enrollment is. If you live in an average city, and have an average tuition rate of $200 a week, and you spend $2,000 on staff development, it takes only three children to enroll for one month to be able to offset that cost.

You know you're not going to run your center 100 percent all the time. By being able to have positive environments for staff, they're going to want to come back. The parents touring are going to want to come back and enroll. That's going to help you in the long run.

Julie: That's really powerful to digest. You have to think about the lifetime value, as you were saying. If a staff member leaves, takes three or four children with him or her, that's a big profit loss. At the same time, if you have people who are raving fans, they're helping you get people into slots. That's a huge gain for you. It's about getting to that point, which is really critical. A lot of times we could be doing all the marketing correctly, getting lots of people in through the door. But then I've also had a lot of clients whose parent turnover rates are very high. They come in, stay for a month or two, and then they're gone. You think about all the expense you put out to market to those parents and families, and now they just leave.

Ty: Right. You can have a fancy website, and you can have a very glossy brochure, and you can have a nice smile when somebody walks in the front door. But at the end of the day, if they go online to Yelp or other sources like that, and read that the last fifteen reviews are awful because the staff are really unhappy, and the parent pulled out after a week because their child came home with a soiled diaper, you're not going to get others to enroll. Perception isn't always reality, but it's very important to recognize that keeping your existing staff and existing families happy is the most important way to market your center. It doesn't come down to all those other things, like I said—the website or the brochure. People can write all sorts of things that sound good. It comes down to the perception. Many, many families rely on their friends, their neighbors, people they know, when it comes to enrolling in a child care center. They also rely on the Internet, and they rely on looking at reviews and trying to understand what other people who have used a program write. People don't always write negative things. They write a lot of positive things that they're very excited about. They'll be very blunt about it.

Julie: Absolutely. That's what we hear a lot of people saying. I asked parents to write reviews, and I was so surprised about the positive things that came out. Keep that in mind. Feedback is not always negative.

Ty: I think I have spent an entire career actively listening to staff and directors and parents, and trying to grow personally and professionally, and evolve what I was doing through that. I think there's a lot of quotable people in my career who have given me a lot of really good knowledge, who have helped me to get to this point where I'm at now.

Julie: Let me ask you this. What is it that went through your mind when you decided to go from one center to three? Or was it just something that just happened? Perhaps you went with the flow and before your knew it, you got up to twenty programs?

Ty: I think early on, when we opened the second program, it was because we actually wanted to create career opportunities for the people in the first program. We thought to ourselves, *We have some amazing people we recruited in this one preschool. I'm sure we have some people who might be assistant director or director qualified in a year. Why don't we create another program?* We were trying to focus on staff retention. Then we quickly filled that program. I think what happened was we grew organically. In other words, we didn't buy any other preschools. People came to us over time and said, "You have a great reputation in the community. We have an opportunity here. Would you be interested in putting a proposal in?" Ordinarily we won those proposals. That's how we then ended up growing and growing.

At some point, when we got to about six or seven, or maybe even eight, programs, I finally left my other job. I was working eighty hours a week when I was very young. I think the one thing I didn't mention to all of you is that I was twenty-three, twenty-four years old. I was, I think, appropriately naïve. I think sometimes when you have too much reality in your life, you might not take the risks that I took. I was very willing to take the risk at the time. I had a very strong belief system that we were doing the right thing. So when we went from eight to twenty, really I think it was because it felt right. It felt like the right partner. We could still do really good things for families. And we didn't feel like, because we were growing, that we were somehow risking the first couple of programs. We invested the same amount of time and resources in those staff. If you decide to grow your business, don't lose sight of the people and the families in the programs that you have already opened. They're equally important.

Julie: Growing that quickly, was there a way that you found was really golden to you to attract staff? Was it, again, that you built it and they came? Or were there different efforts you had to put into place?

Ty: I think the most important thing that we did with our staff was to create an environment where we compensated them on the higher end of the scale. We just made sure that we could accomplish that. We invested in them. Some of you might think, *If I put money into my teachers, I'm going to make less money.* You're incorrect. Let's just do the math. Here's the quick math formula. If you're operating at 72 percent, and you're paying your staff $8 an hour, or if you're operating at 90 percent because you decided to increase your scale to $12 an hour, and are getting better teachers, what do you think is the better business to run? Very simply, the center that is at 90 percent and paying your staff $12 an hour. The incremental amount, the difference between the two of those, does not equal the amount of additional children you're getting. Go back to what I said earlier. If you're getting $800 a month from a family, that's almost $10,000 a year in additional revenue. That's the reason you want to pay staff more. You want to be able to increase your occupancy. It does correlate in almost every state that I've operated child care centers, in every environment, that the more you pay your staff, the longer they're going to stay. The longer they stay, the higher your occupancy. The higher your occupancy, the more money you make. That's how it works.

Julie: Fantastic math. Love those equations. Where did you find the staff? Did you just put the word out there, and you believe, because of the model you built, they came?

Strategy 11

Let staff help recruit staff.

Ty: I think we encourage staff to recruit staff. A lot of staff had friends who had been in similar classes with them. They said, "Come join the CCLC family." We referred to our centers as a family. We never really talked about it as a corporation or anything like that, because that didn't sound very supportive or nurturing. We did talk about family a lot. A lot of them wanted to join the CCLC family. Because the staff are really happy, they recruit their own. They want people to work with them. They bring their friends. Finding staff was not a problem. The other way to recruit staff, when we were opening big centers, is we had recruiting fairs. I opened one of the largest preschools in the United States, with four hundred children. We opened with three hundred sixty, so we had to hire eighty staff within a month and a half. Imagine that challenge. We had recruiting fairs and brought people together on a Saturday morning, because obviously staff work and they're tired after they go home at night. We had a fun event on a Saturday morning, where applicants could engage with our teachers and get to know people that way. That's a very powerful way to recruit staff, if you have to hire a whole bunch at the same time.

Julie: Make it fun and attract them—that's fantastic. What child care program was that? Do you mind sharing?

Ty: It's the Cisco child care center. It's 40,000 square feet. It serves a population of 25,000 employees. They have two child care centers onsite in Silicon Valley. The organization I own still operates it. In fact, I visited it a few weeks ago just to say hello. It's still an amazing program.

Julie: That's wonderful. This has been a fantastic interview, lots of great information. Is there anything you would like to say in closing that maybe we haven't gotten to, or that you would just like our readers to know about you?

Ty: People have asked me over the years why I am in this field, and what is it that really motivates me to be in this field. I believe that if you have a strong passion for children, and you have also a motivation to create a positive setting for staff, you will do that by creating an environment that allows for that to occur. Those are my primary motivators, and I like watching people evolve, the staff evolve. I really enjoy people development. I enjoy the fact that my career has been about watching children, during their formative years, get the education that they need to be able to move on. Those are my two career drivers. Of course, I'm going to be in early childhood education. I'm going to want to hire great staff, pay them a lot of money and have them evolve. That's a natural fit. I hope, if you are in this field, that you share a passion for children, and that you also want to create an environment for staff that's positive. Think about the legacy you're going to leave. Also, you can make a lot of money doing this, by having those full centers we talked about.

To hear this interview in its entirety, go to **www.ChildCareBusinessSuccess BookVault.com**. The password is **RockMyChildCare.com**.

Dream Big—The
Journey Continues

One question I love to ask my audiences is: *What do you really want?* As simple as this question is—it's a very thought-provoking question to answer. Whether you're new in the child care industry or very seasoned like many of my clients, there's always a destination you want to travel to. The problem is we don't often take time to gain clarity and think about the answer to this question: *What do I really want?*

It's your opportunity right now to step into a big space in your life and dream big. This book is filled with stories of people who dreamed big to make magic happen in their child care programs and in their lives and I hope through reading this book you're inspired to take the steps required to bring your dream to life and take what might appear to be impossible and make it possible. It's been my honor to be a part of these stories and to share them with you.

FREE Gifts From Julie Bartkus!

If you're at a place where you need help bringing your BIG, BOLD, DREAMY vision to life, I encourage you to reach out to me for a FREE Discovery Coaching Session at 1.800.211.5671 or at **www.ChildCareBusinessSuccess.com**. You might be just one conversation away from getting the results that you desire and most importantly deserve! Gift Number 2: Grab a FREE copy of my *Child Care Business Success* Magazine at **www.MagazineByJulieBartkus.com**. You can also find me on Facebook at: **www.Facebook.com/ChildCareBusinessSuccess** and LinkedIn at: **www.linkedin.com/in/juliebartkus/**.

I strongly encourage you to visit each one of our sponsors featured in the next section of this book. They helped me bring this publication to life and I am very grateful that now this book is in your hands and available to child care owners and directors worldwide. They are here to support your child care business success. Their stories are also featured on the special website we have set up for the book: **www.ChildCareBusinessSuccessBookVault.com**. The password is: **RockMyChildCare.com**.

In closing, I would like to state that I believe this industry is an absolutely amazing one to be a part of. You have the opportunity to impact many lives in many ways and to leave a legacy that will extend far beyond your immediate reach and far beyond your years here on this planet.

Much Love and Big Hugs,

About the Author

Julie with her niece Ashley Renz. Photo by Salli Renz.

Julie Bartkus is an internationally known Child Care Business Success mentor, speaker and author who helps child care owners and directors create their positive, productive and profitable child care businesses through her on-site customized programs, her publications and her groundbreaking Child Care Program of Excellence Club and Mentorship.

Julie is known for her personalized approach in helping her clients achieve the levels of success they desire, including filling enrollments in record time, transforming workplace culture and attracting and retaining DREAMY staff and clients. She is quickly able to access the problems child care leaders are experiencing and helps them gain clarity as to what their next best steps are so they can experience results in record time, like Mary, who got 36 enrollments in three weeks; or Cheryl, who grew her child care business by 33 percent in sixty days; or Cindy, who is now attracting DREAMY staff.

Your child care program is your baby. Julie meets you where you are and helps you take your personal and professional success to a whole new realm of possibilities.

Your Success Rolodex

On the following pages you'll meet our sponsors. These are people who are passionate about your Child Care Business Success!

5 Enrollment Myths Keeping You from Full Enrollment

Chuck Gibbs

MYTH 1

ALL I NEED IS
MORE INQUIRIES.

 ChildCareCRM

While more inquiries can help, most of the time directors seeking more inquiries are not nurturing the leads they already have. Our average client receives approximately 20 leads a month. If you are relying only on families that "float to the top" and enroll without any effort, you are missing a tremendous opportunity. Through timely and effective follow-up, along with proper tour techniques and asking for the enrollment, directors can convert a much larger percentage of the leads they are already getting.

ChildCareCRM helps you manage and close the leads you already have.

What our customers have to say...

"Childcare CRM is one of the best marketing tools you will ever find! It helps guide directors through the sales process and holds them accountable. The metrics are fantastic and we added nearly $400,000 in the first year."

... Julie Thorner, CEO, Mini University

"Our experience has been phenomenal! The program is so well thought out and industry specific. Our director response has been fantastic and we've definitely seen positive growth in our conversion success rates."

... Michelle Rees, VP of Operations, Kiddie Academy

ChildCareCRM
CUSTOMER RELATIONSHIP MANAGEMENT SPECIFICALLY BUILT FOR CHILD CARE

Serving over 4,000 centers in the United States, Canada, Australia, New Zealand, the United Kingdom

MYTH #2... TIMING DOESN'T MATTER IF I'M THE RIGHT CENTER FOR THEM.

Today's child care consumers want what they want immediately... and it's all about "me." How long are you willing to wait to hear back from someone when you are the consumer? Chances are that after a few hours or certainly a single day, you are on to the next company that will respond to you. By not getting back to your inquiries within the first few hours, if not immediately, you have the potential to lose a lot of business. If you wait a day or two to respond, parents may already be taking a tour of your competition and enrolling elsewhere before you have had a chance to engage them. According to Geary PMG, a leading education advertising agency, 93% of parents start their search online and prospective parents fill out an average of 3.5 inquiry forms when researching early childhood education. Schools that compete for enrollments know that speed to contact matters. Data from our clients show that time to engage and tour is a significant indicator of enrollment success. Those contacted within the first few minutes of their inquiry are four times more likely than average to enroll. This advantage plummets as time stretches on, and after a couple hours the advantage is minimal. Speed matters!

"Being second is to be the first of the ones who lose."

"Child Care CRM saves my management staff so much time. All the information is right at our fingertips wherever and whenever we need it. This is so much faster and efficient!"

... Jennifer Duffield, Owner, Dancing Moose Child Care

"Child Care CRM is great! We are opening two new centers and we should be opening with more enrollments than ever before with our new schools."

... Tom Wiley, Director of Operations, Educational Playcare

ChildCareCRM keeps you on task and on time and prevents leads from falling through the cracks.

MYTH #3... MY BEST DIRECTOR CAN ENROLL ANYONE.

The greatest single factor an owner can hope to control is the conversation that his team has with potential parents inquiring about the school. The vast majority of center managers are educators and not "salespeople" and they just don't inherently understand how a great sales process works. Directors and their staffs need to build connections through understanding the parents' needs and then focusing on those needs. Using great questioning techniques and then incorporating that information into building a relationship with the parents by focusing on those needs will end up building more trust than those who don't. And... people buy from those they trust most. **ChildCareCRM promotes best enrollment practices and lets you easily track and recall information about parents and children along the enrollment journey so everyone is on the same page.**

"I love Child Care CRM! It helps keep me on track regarding who to follow up with, who to call and who wants to tour. And it got our enrollment up and we are now on a waitlist!" ... Debbie Webb, Owner, Kids 'R' Kids Learning Academy

For More Information or to Schedule a Demo:
Call 866-306-1985 or go to www.ChildCareCRM.com

MYTH #4... THERE'S NEVER GOING TO BE AN EASY WAY TO KNOW EXACTLY WHAT'S WORKING.

No two enrollments ever look the same. Some can be a long and complicated process of relationship building while others seem to happen within the first few minutes of the family walking in the door. For those that don't enroll, there may be specific points in the cycle where things go wrong and the family walks away. At every step in the enrollment cycle, you want to be able to keep track of information so that you can use it to improve your results. Some key metrics that you should know are: Who are your current opportunities? Where are your leads coming from? What are your inquiry and tour conversion rates? Why are you losing business and to whom? What are your enrollment trends telling you over time?

ChildCareCRM provides robust reporting that provides the information you need to make better business decisions.

MYTH #5... WE CAN EFFECTIVELY MANAGE OUR LEADS THE WAY WE ALWAYS HAVE WITH PAPER, CARD SYSTEMS OR SPREADSHEETS AND I DON'T KNOW OF ANYTHING AFFORDABLE THAT'S BETTER.

While many business owners believe that all their inquiries are being followed up timely and "worked" by their staff, our studies show quite the opposite for the majority of centers. Simply sending an email or leaving a voicemail message and hoping a prospect calls back is not doing the job. You are leaving a tremendous amount of opportunity on the table that your competitors are grabbing. It's virtually impossible to do a great job with timely following up with parents and providing the experience they would expect with a manual system — and there is no easy way to monitor activity, hold people accountable and obtain the timely feedback you need to be as successful as you can.

ChildCareCRM is quick to set up and easy to use with world-class support. We help manage your entire sales process which saves your staff time, elicits accountability, gives you key metrics to manage your business and provides the parent with a better experience, which means more enrollment!

"The best thing about CRM is the awesome technical support! I love that you listen to suggestions and I can honestly say that I have never had IT support on anything like I have had with this program!" ... **Gina Emch, Owner, Valley Learning Centers**

"I have had 20 years' experience in the child care industry and just wish I could have found a system like ChildCareCRM a lot sooner. It's just awesome." ... **Sindye Alexander, Owner, Munchkin Manor Child Care**

ChildCareCRM
CUSTOMER RELATIONSHIP MANAGEMENT
SPECIFICALLY BUILT FOR CHILD CARE

Serving over 4,000 centers in the United States, Canada, Australia, New Zealand, the United Kingdom

www.ChildCareCRM.com   866-306-1985

EZCare Online Child Care Software, The Easiest Way to Manage Your Workday

"We now spend less than an hour to do what used to take more than a whole day!"

-Tiffany Harmon
Columbus Montessori
Education Center

Only EZCare is backed by 30+ years of knowledge developing software for the childcare community while delivering....

- Cutting edge technology as easy as your iPhone™.
- Tools to connect with parents, saving you time and making them happy.
- Access to your data 24 x 7 on every device.
- Five-star, customer support a phone call away.

The Child Care Community's Leading Support Team

When you get EZCare, you'll also benefit from our 30+ years of experience helping child care centers grow. Our support team consistently achieves customer satisfaction ratings far above software industry standards. In fact, our first client from back in 1985 is still a happy user.

ChildCareIRiS

SCHEDULE THE *RIGHT TEACHER*,
IN THE *RIGHT PLACE*,
AT THE *RIGHT TIME*.

Introducing
ChildCareIRiS

Intelligent Resource iScheduler

The only dedicated scheduling solution for the childcare industry.

ChildCareIRiS is a useful, cloud-based application that is designed to support child care providers by easing common staffing pain points so providers can focus on operating their high-quality programs more efficiently.

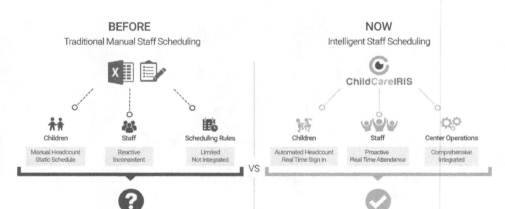

BEFORE				NOW		
Traditional Manual Staff Scheduling				Intelligent Staff Scheduling		
				ChildCareIRiS		
Children	Staff	Scheduling Rules		Children	Staff	Center Operations
Manual Headcount Static Schedule	Reactive Inconsistent	Limited Not Integrated	VS	Automated Headcount Real Time Sign In	Proactive Real Time Attendance	Comprehensive Integrated

Show Child Head Count and Staff in 15-minute Intervals

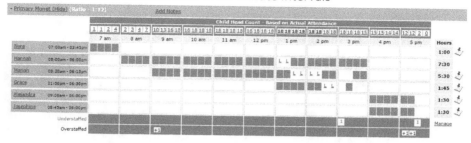

Show Proposed Daily Schedule by Staff...

Ready to Publish, Print and Handout to Staff...

Published Staff Work Schedule
Week of June 5 - June 10, 2017

Office	June 5 Monday	June 6 Tuesday	June 7 Wednesday	June 8 Thursday	June 9 Friday
Annaleen Encina	07:00 AM - 06:30 PM	07:00 AM - 06:30 PM	07:00 AM - 06:30 PM	07:00 AM - 06:30 PM	07:00 AM - 06:30 PM
Grace Jeng	03:30 PM - 04:00 PM	03:30 PM - 04:00 PM	03:30 PM - 04:00 PM	03:30 PM - 04:00 PM	03:30 PM - 04:00 PM
Melissa Wyant	07:00 AM - 06:30 PM	07:00 AM - 06:30 PM	07:00 AM - 06:30 PM	07:00 AM - 06:30 PM	07:00 AM - 06:30 PM
Alejandra Llamas	05:30 PM - 06:00 PM	05:30 PM - 06:00 PM	05:30 PM - 06:00 PM	05:30 PM - 06:00 PM	05:30 PM - 06:00 PM
Jea Sevilla	04:00 PM - 04:30 PM	04:00 PM - 04:30 PM	04:00 PM - 04:30 PM	04:00 PM - 04:30 PM	04:00 PM - 04:30 PM
Amanda Wagner	04:00 PM - 04:30 PM	04:00 PM - 04:30 PM	04:00 PM - 04:30 PM	04:00 PM - 04:30 PM	04:00 PM - 04:30 PM
Josephine Sayson	03:00 PM - 03:30 PM	03:00 PM - 03:30 PM	03:00 PM - 03:30 PM	03:00 PM - 03:30 PM	03:00 PM - 03:30 PM
Mariah Sanchez	03:00 PM - 03:30 PM	07:00 AM - 06:30 PM 03:00 PM - 03:30 PM	03:00 PM - 03:30 PM	07:00 AM - 06:30 PM 03:00 PM - 03:30 PM	03:00 PM - 03:30 PM

Contact us
www.childcareiris.com

info@childcareiris.com

1-877-346-3006

REQUEST A LIVE DEMO

WatchMeGrow
Anywhere.

America's #1 Streaming Video Service for Childcare

INCREASE ENROLLMENT AND RETENTION

Share your story on your website and Facebook with a friendly, animated video

Impress touring parents with a flatscreen WatchMeGrow TV in your lobby

Upgrade to HD for a crisp, full-screen video – the largest in the industry

Trusted by Hundreds of Locations Across the U.S. and Canada

" The best investment we made in our academy.
Pin On Lo, Center Owner , Framingham, MA

" Fantastic. WatchMeGrow simply delivers a better experience.
Bart Sutherin, Center Owner, Clermont, FL

" Over 250 people use it, and everyone is always so pleased!
William Riley, Center Owner, Lubbock, TX

" One of the most successful marketing programs we have.
Rob Waszazak, Center Owner, Delran, NJ

1-800-483-5597 | grow@watchmegrow.com

CHILDCARE MARKETING

Power Web Videos creates and produces content marketing videos to educate and engage potential parents searching for a pre-school.

Our Emmy® award-winning team takes a strategic approach in creating one-on-one video stories that help bring your school to life online and through social media.

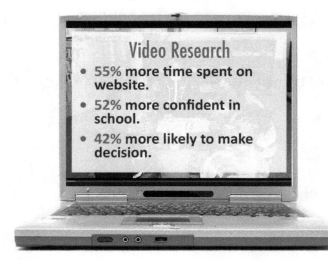

Video Research

- **55% more time spent on website.**
- **52% more confident in school.**
- **42% more likely to make decision.**

VIDEO PACKAGE
Five Videos:
- Owners Website Welcome
- Parent Testimonials
- Tour of School
- Programs
- School Specific

Additional Services:
- Video Search Engine Optimization
- YouTube Channel
- Custom QR
- Mobile Landing Page (for Smartphones)

Contact: Regent Ducas
972.322.9184
rducas@powerwebvideos.com

www.powerwebvideos.com

Scan for Video Examples

POWER WEB VIDEOS
— A VIDEO STRATEGY COMPANY —

CHILDCARE CLIENTS

"Regent immediately captured the philosphy of our company and created videos that truly represented our passion for early care and education. He is professional and knowledgable in his field and we value the high quality videos he created. We look forward to work with him again in the future."
-Karen Lampe and Eric Burdick, Creative World of Childcare, Dayton, OH

"Regent's expertise in content video marketing has given us an online edge when parents are searching for our services. I highly recommend Regent and his crew."
-Michael Williamson, Kids R Kids, Wake Forest, NC

Regent and his team were very easy to work with, they made us feel comfortable and at ease. The best part are the results. The quality of videos and production are excellent.
-Sam Grant, Summit Kids Academy, Lake Worth, FL

Thank you! We are loving the website and videos. We definitely achieved our goal with the videos on shining a light on who is "behind SpringStone". It's making a difference and we are getting a lot of inquiries through the site. Thanks for doing such a great job with the videos!
-Scott Knight, SpringStone Montessori, Las Vegas, NV

"I have seen a significant increase in traffic on our website and an increase in enrollment since we had Regent produce the videos" Your team made the process much easier and enjoyable than we thought it would be."
-Lonnie Hutson, Kids R Kids, Sugarland, TX

*Mention this ad and receive an additional free video with paid package (value $700.00)

All major credit cards accepted

LOVE OUR SERVICE...
SoTellUs™
COLLECT · MARKET · MONETIZE YOUR REVIEWS

Step One Get 5 Star Customer Reviews Instantly

Get the most powerful customer reviews possible by capturing them on video! Using our proprietary app you can collect Video, Audio, or Written reviews from your customers in less then 30 seconds.

Step Two

Your Best Marketing Automated For You

All you have to do is get the review and then SoTellUs takes care of the rest. Your 4 and 5 star customer reviews immediately show up on your website. You don't have to do anything, this process is automated.

Step Three

The Social Proof Your Company Needs

Its not enough to just have a website these days. You need to be in front of your clients where they are hanging out, Social Media! With SoTellUs thats as easy as clicking a button. You can easily share these powerful customer reviews to your social media sites. You get to choose which reviews you share with one simple click.

Step Four What Do Potential Customers See When They Google You?

Esmerio's Master Carpet Care, Inc. has 4.9 out of 5 stars on S...
https://sotellus.com/reviews/esmerios-master-carpet-care-inc/ ▾
★★★★★ Rating: 4.9 - 19 votes
Jose was amazing! My carpets look brand new (even better than new)! They are so old and had so many stains and Jose was able to get them all out. Joseph ...

Tim P gave Esmerio's Master Carpet Care, Inc. 5 out of 5 star...
https://sotellus.com/reviews/esmerios-master-carpet-care-inc/a1h9f7q9/ ▾
★★★★★ Rating: 4.9 - 19 votes
Business Description. Our services include carpet cleaning, upholstery cleaning, tile and grout cleaning, and water damage restoration And our motto is "we ...

Debra B gave Esmerio's Master Carpet Care, Inc. 5 out of 5 st...
https://sotellus.com/reviews/esmerios-master-carpet-care-inc/mta438km/ ▾
★★★★★ Rating: 4.9 - 19 votes
Esmerio Carpet Care is excellent. Jose not only cleans your carpet but, he explains what he is doing and the rational for the process. He is very knowledgeable ...

Esmerio's Master Carpet Care Inc. - Rancho Cucamonga, Cal...
www.facebook.com › ... › Carpet Cleaner ▾
Esmerio's Master Carpet Care Inc., Rancho Cucamonga, California. 3 likes. Local Business

Thanks to sites like Google and Amazon potential customers will research you and make a decision before they ever talk to you. When they search for your business online what are they finding? Luckily with our system when people search for your business your SoTellUs reviews can show up multiple times on the top of the search engines proving to those potential customers that you are the best company to do business with.